John 8:36

Amazing Grace
✦ ADDICTION BIBLE STUDY ✦

MICHAEL K. MASON

WESTBOW
PRESS®
A DIVISION OF THOMAS NELSON
& ZONDERVAN

Copyright © 2016 Michael K. Mason.

All rights reserved. No part of this book may be used or reproduced by any means, graphic, electronic, or mechanical, including photocopying, recording, taping or by any information storage retrieval system without the written permission of the author except in the case of brief quotations embodied in critical articles and reviews.

Scripture taken from the Holy Bible, NEW INTERNATIONAL VERSION®. Copyright © 1973, 1978, 1984, 2011 by Biblica, Inc. All rights reserved worldwide. Used by permission. NEW INTERNATIONAL VERSION® and NIV® are registered trademarks of Biblica, Inc. Use of either trademark for the offering of goods or services requires the prior written consent of Biblica US, Inc.

This book is a work of non-fiction. Unless otherwise noted, the author and the publisher make no explicit guarantees as to the accuracy of the information contained in this book and in some cases, names of people and places have been altered to protect their privacy.

WestBow Press books may be ordered through booksellers or by contacting:

WestBow Press
A Division of Thomas Nelson & Zondervan
1663 Liberty Drive
Bloomington, IN 47403
www.westbowpress.com
1 (866) 928-1240

Because of the dynamic nature of the Internet, any web addresses or links contained in this book may have changed since publication and may no longer be valid. The views expressed in this work are solely those of the author and do not necessarily reflect the views of the publisher, and the publisher hereby disclaims any responsibility for them.

Any people depicted in stock imagery provided by Thinkstock are models, and such images are being used for illustrative purposes only. Certain stock imagery © Thinkstock.

ISBN: 978-1-5127-4742-3 (sc)
ISBN: 978-1-5127-3251-1 (hc)
ISBN: 978-1-5127-4741-6 (e)

Library of Congress Control Number: 2016910296

Print information available on the last page.

WestBow Press rev. date: 07/29/2016

CONTENTS

Getting Started vii

Unit 1: Amazing Grace, How Sweet the Sound ...
    Understanding the Relationship Between
    Addiction and Sin

Lesson 1: Addiction Is Sin 1
Lesson 2: God and Sin in the Bible 6
Lesson 3: Sin and Sacrifice in the Bible 12
Lesson 4: Fundamentals of the Gospel 19

Unit 2: That Saved a Wretch Like Me ...
    Discovering the Relationship between
    Jesus and Sin

Lesson 5: Jesus Becomes Our Sacrifice 27
Lesson 6: Jesus (the) Christ 34
Lesson 7: Jesus and Freedom 41
Lesson 8: The Simplicity of Salvation 46

Unit 3: I Once Was Lost, But Now I am Found ...
    Recognizing the Relationship between
    the Holy Spirit and Sin

Lesson 9: The Holy Spirit 55
Lesson 10: The Spirit and Self-Control 61
Lesson 11: Faith and Deliverance 67
Lesson 12: Fighting the Battle 74

Unit 4: I Was Blind, but Now I See!
    Winning the Spiritual Battle Against
    the Devil and Sin

Lesson 13: The Enemy 82
Lesson 14: Weapons of War 89
Lesson 15: Addiction and Obedience 95
Lesson 16: Addiction and Judgment 101

Prayer of Salvation.. 107

GETTING STARTED

So if the Son sets you free, you will be free indeed.

—John 8:36

Addiction is commonly viewed as a brain disease that has the ability to control the behavior and corrupt the minds of millions of so-called "addicts" worldwide. The recovery industry reinforces this belief by viewing addiction as a disease characterized by a loss of control over behavior, with a biological cause that is independent of choice. Accordingly, the addictive substance is believed to alter the brain's chemistry in such a way as to make it irresistible to the user. Simply put, this popular theory claims that drugs, like opiates and alcohol, have the intrinsic ability to turn a voluntary user into an involuntary one.

This much-acclaimed theory is based primarily on the assumption that addicts are physically unable to resist the call of addictive chemicals. They are allegedly stricken from birth with this condition and are helpless in the fight against the self-destructive symptoms of the so-called disease. In fact, the National Institute on Drug Abuse (a government-funded addiction research center) has stated that addiction is "a brain disease beyond a reasonable doubt." Most treatment organizations (such as Alcoholics Anonymous) share a similar viewpoint. While they sometimes advocate different approaches to a "cure," they all promote the disease model of addiction.

Surprisingly, the success rate for professional addiction treatment currently rests between 20 and 30 percent. This is a sobering statistic, considering the fact that Americans spend close to $20 billion per year on substance abuse treatment. Nevertheless, this means that seven out of ten Americans who participate in secular recovery programs experience relapse within a short period of time.[1] These underwhelming results beg the question: why doesn't treatment work? More specifically, why are the vast majority of people who are treated professionally for the so-called disease of addiction seemingly not being cured?

The answer to this question undoubtedly lies within the framework of the disease concept itself. For instance, the disease model of addiction introduces an extremely frustrating paradox. According to this theory, so-called addicts are presumed to have failed at recovery because of the quality of their choices. However, the very same theory clearly states that addicts suffer from a disease that supposedly inhibits choice.

Furthermore, a great deal of contemporary research shows that substance abusers are not genetically or biologically different from anyone else. In fact, a growing group of physicians and researchers contend that so-called addicts are simply guilty of making self-destructive choices in response to the commonplace stresses of life. According to this revolutionary new theory, addicts do not suffer from some chronic form of a dependency disease; they deliberately choose to abuse intoxicating chemicals, and they can and do choose to quit.

Some well-known researchers in the field believe that addiction is nothing more than a cry for help by those who feel spiritually unfulfilled. Dr Abraham Twerski of the Hazelden Betty Ford Foundation is one of them: "Most people learn through experience that certain substances provide a sense of gratification. Consequently, addictive thinking can lead people to try to quench this vague spiritual craving through food or drugs or sex. These objects may give some gratification, but they do nothing to solve the basic problem: the unmet spiritual needs."[2]

---

[1] Harold C. Urschel, *Healing the Addicted Brain* (Naperville, IL: Sourcebooks, 2009), 7.

[2] Abraham J. Twerski, *Addictive Thinking* (Center City, MN: Hazelden, 1990), 113.

In other words, a growing number of addiction professionals think that while most substance abusers are searching for spiritual answers, they end up settling for chemical solutions.

This radical new theory drives the discussion of addiction in an entirely new direction. What role does religion play in an understanding of addiction? Furthermore, does current research show any connection at all between religious beliefs and sobriety? Dr. Gene Heyman, an addiction psychologist at Harvard, offers some answers as follows:

> Religious values typically teach self-restraint and sobriety. For those who endorse religious values, this settles the issue. They do not have to weigh either the short or long-term consequences of drug use. Rather, they have to decide whether or not they are religious or whether their religious proscriptions apply to the current situation. These turn out to be simpler decisions than whether or not to have a drink. Thus, the prediction is that differences in adherence to religious values are correlated with differences in drug use. The data support the predictions.[3]

In other words, research affirms that people who embrace religious principles have lower rates of addictions. Dr. Heyman also wrote, "Those who prayed frequently and who endorsed the idea of a God who rewards and punishes reported lower levels of use or dependence on cigarettes and alcohol. The researchers' hunch that religion would play a role in times of stress was also confirmed. According to self-reports, stressful events typically increased smoking and drinking. But for those who strongly endorsed a belief in a spiritual world, there was no stress related increase in drug use."[4]

This is a monumental notion in the study of addiction theory. Simply put, religious people are less likely to be addicts than non-religious people.

---

[3] Gene M. Heyman, *Addiction A Disorder of Choice* (Cambridge, MA: Harvard University Press, 2009), 166.

[4] Heyman, 164.

Similar studies also found that lower rates of addiction were associated with adherence to traditional spiritual values and consistent church attendance.

The value of this information cannot be overstated. Statistically speaking, religious beliefs give people a greater chance of beating or avoiding addiction altogether. But people aren't statistics; they are living, breathing human beings who struggle every day. Nevertheless, the data suggests that if addicts are able to wrap their minds around the concepts of religious enlightenment, they have a much greater chance of achieving permanent freedom from their addictions.

Over the years, I have found the majority of so-called addicts to be rather spiritual people who often proclaim a firm belief in God. They are normally well aware of their flaws and are seriously committed to finding solutions and seeking sobriety. The problem is that while they have a legitimate desire to develop a relationship with God, they simply don't know where to begin.

The *Amazing Grace Addiction Bible Study* has been developed to fill the gap between what addicts want to know about God and what they need to know about the undeniable connection between addiction and spirituality. The primary objective of this program is to offer targeted biblical resources to help substance abusers conquer their stubborn addictive behaviors with divine assistance from God.

This *Addiction Bible Study* is a one-of-a-kind program that attacks the subject of chemical dependency on four major fronts.

Unit 1: Amazing Grace, How Sweet the Sound ...
Understanding the Relationship between Addiction and Sin

The first section of our spiritual journey focuses on defining addiction and revealing its true nature in spiritual terms. The objective of this unit is to understand that in spite of what you've been led to believe, addictive behaviors should be considered not in terms of sickness but rather in terms of sin. Substance abuse as a concept can then be understood within the context of sin and sacrificial living introduced and explained in the Bible.

Unit 2: That Saved a Wretch Like Me …
Discovering the Relationship between Jesus and Sin

The second section begins with a summary of the events that transpired in the birth, life, and death of Jesus Christ. The process of salvation is then examined, with an emphasis on the theology of being *born again* and its tangible benefits in terms of eliminating addictive behaviors. Overall, the objective of this unit is to offer the reader a fuller understanding of the biblical connection between the sin of addiction and the gift of salvation.

Unit 3: I Once Was Lost, But Now I am Found …
Recognizing the Relationship between the Holy Spirit and Sin

The third section of this study begins with a discussion of the Holy Trinity, with a special emphasis on the redemptive powers of the Holy Spirit. The role of this supernatural entity is presented in biblical terms and reinforced with real-world examples of the connection between the Spirit and self-control. Faith and grace are explored as spiritual concepts and emphasized in terms of their relative importance in the daily tug-of-war between sin and obedience to God.

Unit 4: I Was Blind, But Now I See!
Winning the Spiritual Battle against the Devil and Sin

The final section of this Bible study addresses the fact that the fight against addictions (and sin in general) involves a broader understanding of the spiritual forces involved. From a biblical perspective, addictions should be viewed in the context of the ongoing spiritual war waged for the souls of mankind. Substance abusers can learn how to fight this battle by using the armor of God and wielding the sword of the Spirit as an offensive weapon against the opposing dark forces in play. Obedience should be viewed as an asset in this fight, ending in the final, irrevocable judgment of God.

UNIT 1

Amazing Grace, How Sweet the Sound … Understanding the Relationship Between Addiction and Sin

If you do what is right, will you not be accepted? But if you do not do what is right, sin is crouching at your door: it desires to have you, but you must master it.

—Genesis 4:7

LESSON 1

ADDICTION IS SIN

We've all been created by God with the ability to choose our own paths and, by extension, our own behaviors. We are granted free will by our Creator so that we can live uninhibited, selfless lives that are pleasing to Him. The problem is that some of us have trouble moderating our behavior in the context of this unlimited freedom, and we eventually make mistakes. In order to win the spiritual battle against addiction, we need to learn to take charge of our own behaviors in order to avoid the pitfalls that accompany a lifestyle of substance abuse.

A great deal of contemporary research says there is nothing different (biologically or genetically) about so-called "addicts" that condemns them to a lifetime of dependency. There is no evidence whatsoever to support the fact that addiction has an overwhelmingly genetic component. No study has ever discovered any chemical or anatomical abnormalities present in addicts that account for their having developed an addiction. Harvard psychiatrist Dr. Lance Dodes confirms these findings. "The most important finding of research into a genetic role in alcoholism is that there is no such thing as a 'gene for alcoholism.' Nor can you directly inherit alcoholism."[5]

This means that in spite of what you've been told, you are not a slave to chemicals but a willing participant in your own addictive actions. You

---

[5] Lance Dodes, *The Heart of Addiction* (New York: HarperCollins Publishers, 2002), 84.

should embrace this fact and attempt to gain control of your thoughts and actions with divine assistance from God.

Ultimately, addictive behaviors must be understood in the context of sin and not sickness. The problem is that most people prefer to be called sick rather than sinful. The simple change of a few letters takes all the pressure off. We can therefore blame a disease for our failings and justify our destructive behavior in the context of biology rather than choice. This is a predictably human response, but it does little to convince us that we are truly capable of controlling our own behaviors.

God understands the gravity of our relationship with sin. Addictions, like all other sins, were thrust upon us at conception. The actions of Adam and Eve sealed our fate in this regard. Not surprisingly, we all struggle on a daily basis to balance the weight of our sins with the will of our God.

Read It

In preparation for this lesson, read the following Scripture: Exodus chapter 20.

Study It

What Is Sin? Most dictionary definitions and information on the subject define sin as "the deliberate transgression of a religious or moral law."

The Spiritual Definition of Sin: The Bible's definition of sin is a little different. The Hebrew word used in the original translation of the Old Testament for *sin* means to "step across." So in simple terms, to commit sin means to willingly step across the line of acceptable behavior.

The Bottom Line: In effect, sin is all about prioritizing the love of self over the love of God. When we sin, we are essentially worshiping ourselves instead of worshiping God. Addictions (like other sins) are excellent examples of selfish, self-destructive practices that undoubtedly cross the line of acceptable behavior.

What Is Acceptable Behavior? The Ten Commandments, given to Moses in the Old Testament book of Exodus, detailed the ten major concepts for defining acceptable behavior in the ancient world. It is no coincidence that the very first commandment handed down by God involved putting him first in our lives. "I am the Lord your God … You shall have no other gods before me" (Exodus 20:2-3).

Addiction and Idolatry: God continued with a second commandment. "You shall not make for yourself an image in the form of anything in heaven above or on the earth beneath or in the waters below. You shall not bow down to them or worship them; for I, the Lord your God, am a jealous God" (Exodus 20:4–5).

This second commandment is all about the worship of physical objects and things other than God Himself. In biblical terms, this is known as *idolatry*.

Addiction Is Sin: Spiritually speaking, addiction is nothing more than a deep-seated form of idolatry. Substance abuse is about loving ourselves more than we love God. James 1:13–15 states, "When tempted, no one should say, 'God is tempting me.' For God cannot be tempted by evil, nor does he tempt anyone; but each person is tempted when they are dragged away by their own evil desire and enticed. Then, after desire has been conceived, it gives birth to sin; and sin, when it is full-grown, gives birth to death."

Addiction in the Scriptures: Since hallucinogenic narcotics are a relatively recent invention, the Bible speaks most often on the subject of addiction in terms of drinking and drunkenness. The apostle Paul wrote to the members of the church in Ephesus, "Therefore do not be foolish, but understand what the Lord's will is. Do not get drunk on wine, which leads to debauchery. Instead, be filled with the Spirit" (Ephesians 5:17–18).

Solomon, the famous son of King David, also wrote, "Wine is a mocker and beer a brawler; whoever is lead astray by them is not wise" (Proverbs 20:1).

Those passages indicate that the primary problems with drinking (and, by extension, drugs) are issues of obedience and self-control.

You Are Not Alone: The good news is that the Bible says we are all sinners as a result of having been born into this world. We are each deemed guilty in God's eyes and in need of redemption from the minute we take our first breaths. The apostle Paul expressed it best when he wrote, "For all have sinned and fall short of the glory of God" (Romans 3:23).

Understand It

As human beings, we are made up of both positive and negative elements of character. The important thing to decide is which side will dominate our lives. Addiction is undoubtedly a sin, but it is not unlike many other sins we face. Any substance we worship has become an object of sin, and therefore our desire for it must be subdued in spiritual terms.

Sin and obedience to God are polar opposites. Our tendency toward sin is often discussed in biblical terms as a desire to please the *flesh,* while the concept of obedience is described in terms of pleasing the *Spirit.* Our flesh is concerned mostly with the pleasures of this world, while the Holy Spirit within us focuses our attention on the principles of righteousness. These two are in a constant tug-of-war for dominance over us.

Regardless of the opinions of others, you are not required to use drugs and alcohol. No one has a gun to your head, forcing you to take the next hit of heroin or to chug the next beer. Your mind may want the substance, but your capacity to exercise free will and choice has the veto power. As an addict, you need to learn to focus your mind on God—not chemicals—in order to subdue your stubborn cravings for the seductive, forbidden fruit of intoxication.

Think About It

1. How much of a role does spirituality play in your real-life struggles with addictive behaviors?

2. Do you ever feel that people dismiss or reject you because you've been labeled an *addict?* Similarly, have you personally ever used the disease theory as an excuse to continue addictive behaviors?

3. Were you aware of the correlation between spirituality and sobriety? Understanding that addiction is sin, do you personally believe that God can help you to control addictive behaviors?

Pray About It

As you take time to pray between lessons, here are a few ideas to get you started:

- Ask God to help you understand that your addictions are not the result of biological sickness but of sin.
- Pray that God convicts you to commit some time and thought to the Scriptures in this study.
- Thank God that He has brought you this far in life and that He has the power to help you conquer your self-destructive, addictive behaviors.

LESSON 2

GOD AND SIN IN THE BIBLE

It is for freedom that Christ has set us free. Stand firm, then, and do not let yourselves be burdened again by a yoke of slavery.

—Galatians 5:1

God does not require us to follow Him; instead, He invites us to do so. Through the Scriptures, He illuminates the divergent paths of obedience and disobedience in our lives. Although He discourages improper behavior, God's love is unconditional—whether or not we follow His directions. Ultimately, we are all granted the freedom to choose our own paths.

Having been conceived in sin, we must conquer the overwhelming urge to place our own desires in a position of prominence and power. Essentially, we must learn to deny the voracious appetites of self in order to subdue our addictions. As humans, we most often worship at the "church of me" by spending all our time and effort desiring the things to which we assign the greatest value. We bow down to their power and influence instead of turning control of our actions over to God.

Beginning with Genesis, the first five books of the Bible were written by Moses and other unnamed authors sometime between the years of 1500–1400 BCE. In order to understand the concept of sin and sacrifice in the Old Testament, we will begin with a brief overview of the text.

Once we've established a foundation of knowledge, we can then begin to understand the benefits of a life dedicated to worshiping God instead of intoxicating chemicals.

Read It

In preparation for this lesson, read the following Scripture: Genesis chapters 1, 2, and 3.

Study It

Creation: In the very first chapter of the book of Genesis, God created the heavens and the earth, day and night, vegetation, and all the animals on land and in the sea. He then finished with the creation of humankind in a total of six days. "So God created man in his own image, in the image of God he created him; male and female he created them" (Genesis 1:27).

The first man, Adam, and the first woman, Eve, were placed in the garden of Eden. They lived in harmony with God's creation in the garden where the Lord provided for all of their needs. They were told they could eat fruit from any tree or plant in the garden, with the exception of The Tree of Knowledge of Good and Evil.

The Forbidden Fruit: In the midst of this idyllic environment, Eve was tempted by a serpent (a symbol of the Devil) to question God's instructions. The serpent refuted the claim that eating from the tree would result in death; instead, he told her that she would become like God, knowing good and evil. When Eve saw that the fruit was desirable and pleasing to the eye, she ate it and shared it with Adam. God responded as follows: "So the Lord God banished him [Adam] from the Garden of Eden to work the ground from which he had been taken. After he drove the man out, he placed on the east side of the Garden of Eden cherubim and a flaming sword flashing back and forth to guard the way to the tree of life" (Genesis 3:23–24).

Sin Enters the World: By choosing to eat the fruit, Adam and Eve put their desires above those of God (which is the essence of addiction and sin). Having been expelled from Eden, they went about living their lives and procreating to establish humankind's presence on the earth. Eventually, humanity's sinful nature became so distasteful to God that He could only find a few people on the earth who continued to follow Him. As a result, He decided to cleanse the earth of sin by way of a massive flood, choosing only to save a faithful man named Noah and his family to begin anew.

The Covenant: However, as a sign of God's mercy in judgment, the earth became repopulated. Because of humankind's ignorance and his obsession with sin, God turned his attention to the task of redeeming humanity as a whole. God made a covenant with Abram, promising him blessings and generations of descendants in exchange for his faithfulness and obedience. Genesis 17:5–7 states, "No longer will you be called Abram; your name will be Abraham, for I have made you a father of many nations. I will make you very fruitful; I will make nations of you, and kings will come from you. I will establish my covenant as an everlasting covenant between me and you and your descendants after you for the generations to come, to be your God and the God of your descendants after you."

Abraham's Descendants: In ancient times, a covenant was a legal arrangement that defined a formally binding relationship between two parties. In effect, the covenant with Abraham represents God's willingness to exchange spiritual blessings and favor for Abraham's obedience and worship. These promises of God were then passed down to Isaac, one of Abraham's sons. God's covenant was once again extended through Isaac's son, Jacob, and his descendants thrived in the sight of God. Jacob fathered a dozen sons who later become the patriarchs of the famed twelve tribes of Israel.

Jacob's family prospered in the land of Canaan, and their numbers increased. They later migrated to Egypt to escape a devastating famine that had befallen their land. As the Hebrews' presence increased in Egypt, they began to be perceived as a military threat by the Egyptians. In order to avoid potential conflicts, the Egyptians then chose to enslave the Hebrews for more than four hundred years.

The Exodus: Under the Egyptian authority of Pharaoh, the Hebrew people were oppressed almost beyond endurance. God eventually intervened when He called a man named Moses (a Hebrew, who had been found and raised by Pharaoh's sister) to approach Pharaoh and intercede on behalf of the Hebrews in order to bring about their release from slavery. "The Lord said, 'I have indeed seen the misery of my people in Egypt. I have heard them crying out because of their slave drivers, and I am concerned about their suffering. So I have come down to rescue them from the hands of the Egyptians and to bring them up out of that land into a good and spacious land, a land flowing with milk and honey'" (Exodus 3:7–8).

After God used various plagues to secure the release of his people, Moses led between two and three million followers into the Sinai Desert. Pharaoh initially agreed to allow the Hebrews to return to their homeland. However, due to a sudden change of heart, he sent his army in pursuit of them. As the slaves fled, they became trapped between the approaching Egyptian military and the Red Sea. In order to preserve His people God parted the Red Sea, allowing the Hebrews to cross safely on dry land. Under Moses's leadership, the group traveled across the desert to Mt. Sinai where God gave them the Ten Commandments. These were basic laws given to regulate life in the Hebrew community.

Forty Years of Wandering: In fulfillment of His word, God then led His people to a place called Kadesh Barnea on the edge of Canaan, the Hebrew Promised Land. Due to their lack of faith and confidence in God's plan for them to inhabit the land, God banished them to wander aimlessly in the desert wilderness for forty years.

Joshua Conquers Canaan: When Moses and the generation of the unfaithful died, God chose Joshua to take His people across the Jordan River in a campaign to conquer the Promised Land. God said to Joshua, "No one will be able to stand against you all the days of your life. As I was with Moses, so I will be with you; I will never leave you or forsake you. Be strong and courageous, because you will lead these people to inherit the land I swore to their ancestors to give them" (Joshua 1:5–6).

Understand It

The Bible says that Adam and Eve were granted absolute freedom in the garden, but they ultimately chose self-will over God's will. God punished them for their actions by banishing them from the garden of Eden. Consequently, we are all born into sin, carrying the burden of their actions as a weight that is heavy to bear. In this way, sin emerged as a powerful force in the lives of all humankind. We are, therefore, condemned as sinners from conception and are in need of spiritual redemption from the time we take our first breaths.

The good news is that as a so-called "addict," you are not alone. Addiction is a sin, but it is no worse than any other sin. All sins were inherited on behalf of humankind in Eden, so all of us suffer the same condition. You are not an addict; you are just a sinner like everyone else. The apostle Paul summarized it best by saying, "Therefore, just as sin entered the world through one man, and death through sin, and in this way death came to all people, because all sinned—for before the law [the Ten Commandments] was given, sin was in the world" (Romans 5:12).

Think About It

1. Why do you think Adam and Eve decided to disobey God and eat the fruit?

2. Do you agree with the assertion that you have free will and therefore have control over your addictive behaviors? Why or why not?

3. Do you understand being called a sinner is not necessarily a bad thing, considering the fact that we all fall into that category?

Pray About It

As you take time to pray between lessons, here are a few ideas to get you started:

- Ask God to open your mind to a deeper understanding of Scripture.
- Pray that you will begin to comprehend the concepts of sin and sacrifice.
- Thank God for granting you the opportunity to learn about Him and study His Word.

LESSON 3

SIN AND SACRIFICE IN THE BIBLE

The fool says in his heart, "There is no God."

—Psalm 53:1

As we continue our journey of discovery through the books of the Old Testament, a distinct pattern emerges. The story of the ancient Israelites is an excellent example of a predictable cycle of human beings interacting with God. Even though they witnessed many signs and wonders, they never failed to return to their sinful, idolatrous behaviors. They would then cry out to God to save them from a predicament of their own creation.

As sinners and substance abusers, we are often guilty of repeating the very same pattern. We get ourselves into trouble by deliberately disobeying God, and then we cry out for His saving grace. Luckily, God will never forsake us, even though He knows we will probably repeat the cycle. As we work our way through the remaining books of the Old Testament, pay special attention to the growing influence of the widespread sin of idolatry.

Read It

In preparation for this lesson, read the following Scripture: Isaiah chapter 53.

Amazing Grace Addiction Bible Study

Study It

The Monarchy Begins: Around 1000 BCE, rather than trusting the authority of God, the Israelites insisted on installing a monarchy (like those of the surrounding countries) to rule their land. A man named Saul was chosen as the first king of Israel, which consisted of the original twelve tribes—the descendants of Abraham. Saul would eventually turn out to be a mighty warrior but a dreadful king.

Saul Disobeys God: Eventually, Saul deliberately disobeyed God's direct instructions, given through the prophet Samuel. As a result, God rejected him as king over Israel with the following words: "Does the Lord delight in burnt offerings and sacrifices as much as in obeying the Lord? To obey is better than sacrifice, and to heed is better than the fat of rams. For rebellion is like the sin of divination, and arrogance like the sin of idolatry. Because you have rejected the word of the Lord, he has rejected you as king" (1 Samuel 15:22–23).

David and Goliath: Around 1020 BCE, the Israelite and Philistine armies were poised for battle on either side of the Valley of Elah. Rather than have the armies meet in a full-scale battle, the Philistine giant, Goliath, challenged the Israelites to send out a single man to fight him. The victor of this engagement would decide the outcome of the war (a common practice in ancient times). However, none of Israel's soldiers was courageous enough to answer Goliath's boastful challenge. Although David was a mere boy and not yet a soldier in Saul's army, he showed complete faith in God's power by responding to Goliath's arrogant summons and slaying him with a single smooth stone from his slingshot. First Samuel 17:49–50 says, "Reaching into his bag and taking out a stone, he slung it and struck the Philistine on the forehead. The stone sank into his forehead, and he fell face down on the ground. So David triumphed over the Philistine with a sling and a stone; without a sword in his hand he struck down the Philistine and killed him."

David Becomes King: Saul's tumultuous rule was marred by dissension, and the kingdom of Israel eventually became divided. Saul ended up taking his own life in a battle against the Philistines on Mount Gilboa. The former shepherd boy, David, who had grown into a mighty warrior, was chosen by God to replace Saul as king of Israel.

The Temple in Jerusalem: David was a righteous king and ruled justly in Israel for many years. In fact, he was chosen by God to reunite the original twelve tribes and usher Israel into the united kingdom era. Eventually, King David wanted to honor God by building a temple in Jerusalem in which to house the ark of the covenant. However, because David was a man of war, the building of the temple (which symbolized the dwelling place of God) was accomplished by his son, Solomon.

Sacrifice at the Temple: The entire Old Testament sacrificial system, as outlined by Moses in the book of Leviticus, was undertaken at the temple in Jerusalem. The people of Israel were required to regularly atone for their sins by offering gifts and animal sacrifices to the Lord. On the yearly Day of Atonement, the high priest would first sacrifice a bull as an offering to God for his personal sins. He would then present two goats at the door of the temple, with the intent of addressing the corporal sins of the people. One goat would be designated as "the Lord's goat" and offered within the temple as a blood sacrifice. The blood of this slain goat would be sprinkled directly on the "mercy seat," otherwise known as the lid of the ark of the covenant. The other goat, known as the "Azazel" goat, would be figuratively burdened with the sins of all Israel and released into the wilderness, never to return. This symbolic practice, undertaken one day each year, has given rise to the modern term *scapegoat*.

Kingdoms Divide: After Solomon's death, the nation of Israel once again became divided. Around 930 BCE, ten of the original twelve tribes broke away from the rest and came together to form the northern kingdom of Israel. The remaining tribes joined forces in the south to become the southern kingdom of Judah, named for its largest original tribe. This division of the tribes weakened the kingdoms and made them attractive targets for conquest by other nations.

Israel Is Conquered: The sin of idolatry spread like a disease under many of the Israelite kings in the years following Solomon's reign. As a result of the people's disloyalty and sin, God allowed the Assyrian Empire to conquer the northern kingdom of Israel and scatter its inhabitants throughout the world. For similar reasons, God allowed Babylon to capture and destroy the southern kingdom of Judah about 150 years later. Jerusalem and the temple were destroyed, and many of the inhabitants of the city were taken into exile in Babylon. Ezekiel 11:9–12 says, "I will drive you out of the city and deliver you into the hands of foreigners and inflict punishment on you. You will fall by the sword and I will execute judgment on you at the borders of Israel. Then you will know that I am the Lord … For you have not followed my decrees or kept my laws but have conformed to the standards of the nations around you."

The Exile and Return: During the exile, numerous prophets (such as Ezekiel and Daniel) began to predict the resurgence of Israel and the rebuilding of the temple in Jerusalem. Around 500 BCE, the prophet Nehemiah and about fifty thousand others returned to the Holy Land and started resurrecting the city and Israel itself. The walls around Jerusalem were rebuilt, and a second temple was constructed and dedicated to God.

The Prophets: Before the conquest of the northern and southern kingdoms, God appointed a few specific followers as prophets to communicate His wishes to the people. During those years of tumult and constant threat of conquest, the people began hoping for a zealous Messiah to deliver them from the hands of their foreign oppressors.

Messiah: The Anointed One: Messiah means "anointed one" in Hebrew, and it refers to the person whom God would send to earth as a savior or liberator of His people. The Messiah is described in the Bible as a direct descendant of King David; he would come to unite the original twelve tribes of Israel and herald an era of eternal global peace.

Old Testament Messianic Prophecy: There are about sixty different prophecies related to the coming of the Messiah in Old Testament texts. The first of these prophecies was probably written as many as four hundred years before the birth of Jesus, with the last one no less than two hundred years prior to His birth.

The Prophet Isaiah: The book of Isaiah includes some of the most famous and recognizable pieces of messianic prophecy. For instance, Isaiah wrote, "Therefore the Lord himself will give you a sign. The virgin will conceive and give birth to a son, and will call him Immanuel [God with us]" (Isaiah 7:14).

He continued along those lines two chapters later. "For to us a child is born, to us a son is given, and the government will be on his shoulders. And he will be called Wonderful Counselor, Mighty God, Everlasting Father, Prince of Peace" (Isaiah 9:6).

The Messiah Is Coming: The following prophecy is a bit of a departure from the traditional messianic conception, and it points us toward the idea of a more pacifistic deliverer to come. "But he was pierced for our transgressions, he was crushed for our iniquities; the punishment that brought us peace was on him, and by his wounds we are healed … Therefore, I will give him a portion among the great, and he will divide the spoils with the strong, because he poured out his life unto death, and was outnumbered with the transgressors. For he bore the sin of many and made intercession for the transgressors" (Isaiah 53:5, 12).

Understand It

In these Scriptures, we are introduced to the idea of a Messiah who intercedes for us between the manifestation of our sins and God. We now understand that the Old Testament concept of atonement for sin involved a complicated system of gifts and animal sacrifices, regularly made to atone for inappropriate behavior. People would bring lambs, for instance, and present them to the Levite priests at the temple to be sacrificed to God on their behalf. Pouring the animal's blood on the altar was the mechanism by which the entire populace of Israel received forgiveness for their sins.

Isaiah presented one of the first hints that the coming Messiah would satisfy the traditional requirements of the sacrificial instrument by which all would be redeemed. Those writings, most likely completed hundreds of years before the birth of Jesus, pointed in the direction of a new blood covenant that would be offered for the redemption of sin. Indeed, the much-prophesied Messiah would walk the earth hundreds of years later in the form of a man, born of a virgin in an ancient town called Bethlehem.

Think About It

1. What kind of Messiah were the Hebrews expecting to come? What were they expecting him to accomplish for Israel as a whole?

2. Why did God allow foreign enemies to conquer Israel and destroy the temple in Jerusalem? Of which sin were they most guilty?

3. Why is an understanding of the Old Testament sacrificial system important in terms of gaining a deeper understanding of the events described in the rest of the Bible?

Pray About It

As you take time to pray between lessons, here are a few ideas to get you started:

- Ask God to help you comprehend the importance of the Old Testament prophecies about the Messiah.

- Pray that God will help you gain a greater understanding of the obvious connections between the Old Testament and New Testament.
- Thank God for creating in you a genuine desire to read and understand His wishes and His Word.

LESSON 4

FUNDAMENTALS OF THE GOSPEL

I am the resurrection and the life. The one who believes in me will live, even though they die; and whoever lives by believing in me will never die. Do you believe this?

—**John 11:25–26**

Roughly a four-hundred-year gap exists between the end of the Old Testament period and the beginning of the life of Jesus. Scholars most often refer to this as the inter-testament period, which began around 400 BCE. It was a difficult time for the people of Israel because they were constantly fighting through lengthy periods of revolt, and they often endured oppressive foreign occupation. God's people finally fought for and gained their independence from the Macedonian/Greek Empire around 166 BCE. But this period of independence was short-lived as the next great superpower of the ancient world came charging across their borders.

In 63 BCE, the Roman general, Pompey, conquered the Holy Land and took control of the city of Jerusalem. In the process, the Romans massacred priests and defiled the temple, stirring animosity among the occupied Jews. Despite their brutality, the Romans attempted to appease the orthodox sensibilities of the people and avoid rebellion by allowing the continued practice of temple worship in Jerusalem. While their own religion was based on the belief in many different gods, the Romans recognized the importance of maintaining the traditional religious practices of the Jews.

Despite being allowed to worship in accordance with their beliefs, the Jews longed for the promised Messiah to liberate them from the burdens of Roman authority.

Read It

In preparation for this lesson, read the following Scripture: Luke chapters 1 and 2.

Study It

The Virgin Birth: The birth of the prophesied Messiah was proclaimed by the angel Gabriel to a peasant woman named Mary. She had been pledged in marriage to a man named Joseph, a direct descendant of King David. The angel informed Mary that she would conceive a child through the workings of the Holy Spirit.

Joseph Hears from God: Upon learning of Mary's pregnancy, Joseph, a righteous man, decided to divorce her quietly in order to spare her public disgrace. (According to ancient custom, once a couple became engaged, it would take a decree of divorce to end the relationship, even before an actual marriage ceremony took place.) Before Joseph did so, however, an angel of the Lord appeared to him in a dream and told him not to be concerned about proceeding with the marriage. "The angel of the Lord said … 'What is conceived in her [Mary] is from the Holy Spirit. She will give birth to a son, and you are to give him the name Jesus, because he will save his people from their sins'" (Matthew 1:20–21).

The Birth Story: The actual birth took place in a cave or animal pen. Jesus's birth and the declaration of his messiahship were heralded by angels to shepherds in the field. "And there were shepherds living out in the fields nearby, keeping watch over their flocks at night. An angel of the Lord appeared to them, and the glory of the Lord shone around them, and they were terrified. But the angel said to them, 'Do not be afraid. I bring you good news that will cause great joy for all the people. Today in the town of David a Savior has been born you; he is the Messiah, the Lord'" (Luke 2:8–11).

Simeon Recognizes the Messiah: A short time after the birth, Mary and Joseph took Jesus to the temple to present him to the Lord, as was the custom required by Jewish law. When they approached the temple, they were met by a devout Jew named Simeon. Upon seeing Jesus, Simeon proclaimed, "Sovereign Lord, as you have promised, you may now dismiss your servant in peace. For my eyes have seen your salvation, which you have prepared in the sight of all nations: a light for revelation to the Gentiles [non-Jews] and for glory to your people Israel" (Luke 2:29–32).

John the Baptist: A man called John the Baptist, who was of priestly descent, had spent much time in the Jordan River valley preaching baptism [ritual immersion] for the forgiveness of sins. An angel proclaimed that John had come to "prepare the way" for the coming of the Messiah.

The Baptism of Jesus: At about age thirty, Jesus traveled to the shores of the Jordan River to be baptized by his cousin, John. Luke 3:21–22 states, "When all the people were being baptized, Jesus was baptized too. And as he was praying, heaven was opened and the Holy Spirit descended on him in bodily form like a dove. And a voice came from heaven: 'You are my Son, whom I love; with you I am well pleased.'"

The Voice of God: The voice from heaven belonged to God, identifying Jesus as the Messiah, the anointed one. John the Baptist confirmed this notion, saying, "And I myself did not know him, but the one who sent me to baptize with water told me, 'The man on whom you see the Spirit come down and remain is he who will baptize with the Holy Spirit' I have seen and I testify that this is the Son of God" (John 1:33–34).

Jesus Is Tempted: Immediately after His baptism, Jesus withdrew into the wilderness. In the midst of forty days of fasting and praying, He was tempted by the Devil himself. Jesus denied the attempts of Satan, rebuked him three times with Scripture, and emerged victorious to begin the task of spreading the Word of God. "Again, the devil took him to a very high mountain and showed him all the kingdoms of the world and their splendor. 'All this I will give you,' he said, 'if you bow down and worship me.' Jesus said to him, 'Away from me, Satan! For it is written: 'Worship the Lord your God, and serve him only.' Then the devil left him, and the angels came and attended to him" (Matthew 4:8–11).

Gathering Disciples: As His public ministry began, Jesus selected twelve men who became the core group of followers who traveled with Him and studied under His teaching. In one particular encounter, Jesus met two fishermen—Peter and Andrew—near the Sea of Galilee. "'Follow me,' Jesus said, 'and I will make you fishers of men'" (Matthew 4:19 KJV).

Immediately, the two brothers responded by leaving their fishing business and following Him. Similar encounters with the remaining ten disciples followed.

The Sermon on the Mount: Jesus issued his much-acclaimed Sermon on the Mount, as described in the gospel of Matthew, to thousands of followers near Capernaum on the Sea of Galilee. He said, "Ask and it will be given to you; seek and you will find; knock and the door will be opened to you. For everyone who asks receives; the one who seeks finds; and to the one who knocks, the door will be opened" (Matthew 7:7–8).

Miracles: Jesus was not just a dynamic speaker; He was also appointed by God to conduct miracles. The Gospels describe more than thirty different miracles, ranging from healing various illnesses to raising a man named Lazarus from the dead. These miracles served to establish His divinity and authority to the people of the time. On that subject, Jesus stated, "Believe me when I say that I am in the Father and the Father is in me; or at least believe on the evidence of the works themselves" (John 14:11).

Two New Commandments: One of the key teachings of Jesus's earthly ministry lies in the following passage: "Jesus replied, 'Love the Lord your God with all your heart and with all your soul and with all your mind. This is the first and greatest commandment. And the second is like it: Love your neighbor as yourself. All the Law and the Prophets hang on these two commandments'" (Matthew 22:37–40).

The Messiah Has Come: In an early encounter with a Samaritan woman, Jesus actually admitted to His identity as the Messiah. This startling admission to a Samaritan woman was significant because Jews did not normally associate with Samaritans. "The woman said, 'I know that Messiah (called Christ) is coming. When he comes, he will explain everything to us.' Then Jesus declared, 'I, the one speaking to you—I am he'" (John 4:25–26).

One in the Same: In the gospel of John, Jesus also said, "I and the Father are one" (John 10:30).

Understand It

So, instead of avoiding the title *Messiah*, Jesus settled the question altogether by embracing it. In the midst of the Roman occupation of Palestine, it was a very dangerous move to make. Don't forget that the Jews were waiting for a militant, rebellious figure to rise up as Messiah and end the Roman occupation. In His public declaration as Messiah, Jesus was risking His very life.

Jesus's initial public ministry was enthusiastically embraced by the people, but it was greeted with disdain by those in positions of spiritual and political power. As the movement gained momentum, the Jews in power began to bristle with animus and jealousy. They thought, *What right does this small-town preacher have to question our authority? How dare this simple man make proclamations about His authority and power in God's kingdom!* Eventually, these powerful men determined to do anything to undermine Jesus and destroy His following.

Think About It

1. Why is it important for us to believe that Jesus was born as the result of the virgin birth? Why does it matter?

2. Why was it important for Jesus to enter the wilderness for forty days after His baptism? Why was this action necessary?

3. Did Jesus avoid or embrace being called the Messiah?

Pray About It

As you take time to pray between lessons, here are a few ideas to get you started:

- Ask God to help you understand the importance of the real-life story of Jesus.
- Pray that God will help you to fully embrace the Gospels as spiritual history.
- Thank God for loving you enough to arrange for your salvation thousands of years before you were born.

UNIT 2

That Saved a Wretch Like Me ...
Discovering the Relationship
between Jesus and Sin

LESSON 5

JESUS BECOMES OUR SACRIFICE

How much more, then, will the blood of Christ, who through the eternal Spirit offered himself unblemished to God, cleanse our consciences from acts that lead to death, so that we may serve the living God.

—Hebrews 9:14

If we can say with confidence that we understand who Jesus was, we can begin to reconcile His position within the context of Old Testament thinking. Because sin entered the world when Adam and Eve deliberately disobeyed God in the garden of Eden, humankind then lived under the law of Moses for nearly two thousand years, making ritual blood sacrifices to atone for sins. When Jesus (the Messiah) came to earth and sacrificed His blood on the cross, temple sacrifice became obsolete. This means that all our sins have been effectively canceled by the blood offering of Jesus, the aptly-named Lamb of God.

The Gospels make the crystalline case that Jesus was the Son of God. He willingly sacrificed His life to offer atonement for the sins of all of humankind. Jesus confirmed this fact in His own words. "The reason my Father loves me is that I lay down my life—only to take it up again. No one takes it from me, but I lay it down of my own accord … This command I received from my Father" (John 10:17–18).

Instead of continuing the ritual practice of animal sacrifices at the temple, believers need only to accept the one-time, final sacrifice of Jesus for the redemption of their sins.

Read It

In preparation for this lesson, read the following Scripture: Luke chapters 22, 23, and 24.

Study It

Jesus Reveals His Fate: As Christ continued to travel and teach, He began to speak prophetic words about the nature of things yet to come. His disciples stubbornly refused to believe these words and struggled to comprehend the full impact of the events that were about to unfold. Luke 24:7 states, "The Son of Man must be delivered over to the hands of sinners, be crucified and on the third day raised again."

Jerusalem at Passover: In the third year of His public ministry, Jesus and His disciples traveled to Jerusalem to celebrate Passover. On a day that has become known as Palm Sunday, Jesus arrived in the city on the back of a donkey colt. This specific event was prophesied in the Old Testament book of Zechariah around 500 BCE.

Jesus Wrecks the Temple: Once inside the city, Jesus made His way to the temple. Luke described the scene. "When Jesus entered the temple courts, he began to drive out those who were selling. 'It is written,' he said to them, 'My house will be a house of prayer but you have made it a den of robbers.' Every day he was teaching at the temple. But the chief priests, the teachers of the law and the leaders among the people were trying to kill him" (Luke 19:45–47).

Caiaphas: These events raised the profile of Jesus in the minds of the Jewish authorities and their Roman occupiers. The temple priests and the Pharisees feared that Jesus's rise in popularity would affect their relative positions in the sociopolitical setting of the day. The high priest (Caiaphas) began plotting the downfall of Jesus and would stop at nothing to maintain control of his position in the religious and social hierarchy in Jerusalem. He was even quoted in the gospel of John as saying, "You do not realize that it is better for you that one man die for the people than that the whole nation perish" (John 11:50).

The Last Supper: As the week unfolded, Jesus told His disciples to prepare the Passover meal in a room inside the city. Once they had gathered, Jesus performed the ritual known as the Eucharist or the Last Supper. "And he took bread, gave thanks and broke it, and gave it to them, saying, 'This is my body given for you; do this in remembrance of me.' In the same way after the supper he took the cup, saying, 'This cup is the new covenant in my blood, which is poured out for you'" (Luke 22:19–20).

Judas Acts: At this gathering, Jesus told Judas Iscariot (the betrayer) to "do quickly" what he must do. Judas then exited the feast and agreed to deliver Jesus into the hands of the Jewish elite for thirty pieces of silver.

To the Garden: After the Passover meal, Jesus and the remaining eleven disciples made their way to the garden of Gethsemane on the outskirts of Jerusalem. "He withdrew about a stone's throw beyond them, knelt down and prayed, 'Father, if you are willing, take this cup from me; yet not my will, but yours be done.' An angel from heaven appeared to him and strengthened him. And being in anguish he prayed more earnestly, and his sweat was like drops of blood falling to the ground" (Luke 22:41–43).

This is one of the most important points in the gospel narratives. It is the very moment that Jesus made the final decision to give His life as a ransom for all humanity.

Jesus Betrayed: Shortly thereafter, Jesus was identified (with the help of Judas Iscariot) to a militant crowd of priests and temple guards. These men arrested Jesus and took Him before a group known as the Sanhedrin (a version of the Jewish supreme court). At the trial, which took place that same evening, the high priest interrogated Jesus and accused Him of rebellion against God and Jewish law. The gospel of Mark describes one particular exchange. "Again the high priest asked him, 'Are you the Messiah, the Son of the Blessed One?' 'I am,' said Jesus. 'And you will see the Son of Man sitting at the right hand of the Mighty One and coming on the clouds of heaven'" (Mark 14:61–62).

The Verdict: The Jewish elite were enraged by these comments, and Jesus was found guilty of blasphemy and sedition. He was beaten and eventually taken before the ruling Roman governor of Palestine, Pontius Pilate, for sentencing. The accusers brought false charges against Jesus and demanded His death. Pilate eventually complied, sentencing Jesus to die on the cross.

The Crucifixion: In antiquity, Roman crucifixion was a popular means of torture and execution; it was generally reserved for criminals who had committed capital offenses. In fact, death by crucifixion was considered so brutal that a word was created to describe it. The term *excruciating*, which literally means "out of the cross," is derived from this ancient practice. Jesus was nailed to the cross around nine o'clock in the morning. The Bible says that darkness fell on the land around noon on that day, and the sun stopped shining for a while. After a few hours on the cross, Jesus succumbed. John 19:28–30 states, "Later, knowing that everything had now been finished and so that scripture would be fulfilled ... Jesus said, 'It is finished.' With that, he bowed his head and gave up his spirit."

Death: Jesus died a physical death on the cross around three o'clock in the afternoon. His mother, Mary, and others witnessed His passing and helped to take His body down and prepare it for burial. Joseph of Arimathea, a rich man who was a member of the Sanhedrin and a secret follower of Jesus, provided the tomb in which Jesus's physical remains were interred.

The Resurrection: On the morning of the third day, certain women returned to the tomb to prepare Jesus's body for permanent burial. According to Jewish custom, they intended to wash the body and anoint it with spices and perfumes. Luke described the scene. "They found the stone rolled away from the tomb, but when they entered, they did not find the body of the Lord Jesus. While they were wondering about this, suddenly two men in clothes that gleamed like lightning stood beside them. In their fright the women bowed down with their faces to the ground, but the men said to them, 'Why do you look for the living among the dead? He (Jesus) is not here; he has risen!'" (Luke 24:2–6).

Post-resurrection Appearances: In the days following His crucifixion, Jesus made about a dozen post-resurrection appearances to a number of different people. John wrote, "On the evening of the first day of the week, when the disciples were together, with the doors locked for fear of the Jewish leaders, Jesus came and stood among them and said, 'Peace be with you!' After he said this, he showed them his hands and side. The disciples were overjoyed when they saw the Lord" (John 20:19–20).

Doubting Thomas: The first time Jesus appeared to the disciples, one of them, Thomas, was not in attendance. When he returned, Thomas refused to believe that his companions had actually seen Jesus. "A week later his [Jesus's] disciples were in the house again, and Thomas was with them. Though the doors were locked, Jesus came and stood among them and said, 'Peace be with you!' Then he said to Thomas, 'Put your finger here; see my hands. Reach out your hand and put it into my side. Stop doubting and believe'" (John 20:26–27).

The Ascension: Jesus gave specific instructions to His disciples before He ascended to heaven. "Then Jesus came to them and said, 'All authority in heaven and on earth has been given to me. Therefore go and make disciples of all nations, baptizing them in the name of the Father and of the Son and of the Holy Spirit, and teaching them to obey everything I have commanded you. And surely I am with you always, to the very end of the age'" (Matthew 28:18–20).

Understand It

There is no doubt that Jesus had the power to stop the process of His own crucifixion and punish those who conspired to take His life. After all, if He had the power to raise people from the dead, He certainly had the power to save Himself. However, Scripture affirms that He gave His life freely so that you and I might have the opportunity for redemption and eternal life. Ultimately, the sacrificial offering of Jesus (who had no sin) was orchestrated by God in order to reverse the damage done to humankind by Adam and Eve in the garden of Eden.

So what does this mean in the context of addiction? First and foremost, we must accept that addiction is driven by nothing more than behavior and choice. Since sin is most often defined as *crossing the line of acceptable behavior,* addictions must be understood to fall in that category. I think we can all agree that abusing substances is wrong and can thus be categorized as sinful behavior.

Remember that substance abuse is not really worse than any other sins, but it is unquestionably a sin. If we had lived in the time of Moses, we would've been required to offer a blood sacrifice to atone for our sins. But since Jesus did His work on the cross, our sins have effectively been canceled. All we need to do is accept this sacrifice on our behalf. In effect, Jesus traded His death on the cross for the debt of sin we owe in life.

Think About It

1. If Jesus was aware of Judas and his intentions to betray him, why didn't He stop him?

2. What is the importance of Jesus's prayer in the garden of Gethsemane?

3. Can you relate to the apostle who has come to be known as *doubting Thomas?*

Pray About It

As you take time to pray between lessons, here are a few ideas to get you started:

- Ask God to help you understand that the crucifixion and resurrection were necessary for your own personal sanctification.
- Pray that God grants you the faith necessary to avoid being labeled a *doubting Thomas* in spiritual terms.
- Thank God that He sent His only Son to die a horrible death so that you might have eternal life.

LESSON 6

JESUS (THE) CHRIST

The Word [Jesus] became flesh and made his dwelling among us. We have seen his glory, the glory of the One and Only, who came from the Father, full of grace and truth.

—**John 1:14**

Having discussed the events of Jesus's life, we are faced with some interesting questions. For instance, what evidence do we have (outside the Bible) that Jesus actually existed? How confident are we that the accounts written in the Gospels are accurate? And finally, how can we be sure that Jesus was the actual Messiah described in the prophetic books of the Old Testament? Let's deal with these questions one at a time.

First of all, how do we know for certain that Jesus of Nazareth actually existed? Interestingly, one answer to this question lies in the details concerning the authors of the Gospels that tell His story. Of the four Gospels presented in the New Testament, two were written by actual eyewitnesses of the events they described.

The gospel of Matthew was written by a former tax collector who left his job to follow Jesus. This man, also known in the Bible as the "son of Alphaeus," is undeniably the same disciple called Matthew described in the first book of the New Testament. Additionally, the gospel of John was written by another disciple of Jesus known as "John, son of Zebedee."

So it's clear that both Matthew and John were actual eyewitnesses of the events that transpired, which means they wrote their accounts relying on nothing more than their own memories of the events as they occurred. They witnessed many of the miracles being performed, and both saw Jesus in His post-resurrection body.

The books of Mark and Luke were written by close companions of the more famous disciples. The author of the gospel of Mark was an associate of the apostle Peter. Luke (who wrote the gospel that bears his name) was a colleague of the apostle Paul. Both Peter and Paul had personal experiences with Jesus, and together their writings account for more than 70 percent of the material in the New Testament. Therefore, Mark and Luke wrote their gospels based on information provided directly to them by two of the most influential Christians leaders in the history of the early church.

Read It

In preparation for this lesson, read the following Scripture: Colossians chapter 2.

Study It

What's in a Name? The name *Jesus* is an English translation of the Hebrew name *Joshua* (pronounced Ye-shu-a). It is derived from the Hebrew word that means "savior." The term *Christ* is not a name; it is actually a title. The English word *Christ* comes from the Greek word *Christos* which means "Messiah." So Jesus Christ is actually translated more correctly as "Yeshua, the Messiah."

What is the Supporting Evidence? There are about twenty-four thousand ancient manuscripts of the New Testament in existence today. That's a very large number, considering that many of these copies were produced more than nineteen centuries ago. Additionally, the New Testament has survived in a purer form than any other great book from history. The existing copies examined by scholars are said to be 99.5 percent similar in terms of content. In other words, all the copies of the New Testament that have been discovered over the centuries are within half a percent of being identical.[6]

Third-Party Evidence: Jesus is mentioned in the Talmud, a Jewish rabbinical text that emerged around 200 CE. A Roman senator, Tacitus, also spoke of Jesus in his major writings about the reigns of such Roman emperors as Claudius and Nero. Another Roman writer, Pliny, included evidence about Jesus in his many writings. His works were well known in antiquity, as he was actually the governor of ancient Bithynia in northern Turkey. Finally, in his first century work entitled *Antiquities of the Jews,* the famous Jewish historian, Flavius Josephus, wrote, "Now there was about this time Jesus, a wise man, for he was a doer of wonderful works, a teacher of such men as received the truth with pleasure. He drew over to him both many of the Jews and many Gentiles. When Pilate, at the suggestion of the principle men against us, had condemned him to the cross, those who loved him did not forsake him. And the tribe of Christians so named for him are not extinct to this day."[7]

Jesus the Messiah: How do we know that Jesus of Nazareth was the actual Messiah prophesied in the Bible? Remember that there are about sixty different messianic prophecies included in the Old Testament. They present us with more than 250 unique details that were fulfilled in the person of Jesus.

Although the disciples also witnessed many signs and wonders during their time with Jesus, even they were slow to recognize His position as the prophesied Messiah. In the gospel of Luke, Jesus said the following: "How foolish you are, and how slow to believe all that the prophets have spoken! Did not the Messiah have to suffer these things and then enter his glory?" And beginning with Moses and all the Prophets, he explained to them what was said in all the scriptures concerning himself" (Luke 24:25–27).

---

[6] Lee Stroebel, *The Case for Christ* (Grand Rapids, MI: Zondervan, 1998), 65.
[7] Flavius Josephus, *Antiquities of the Jews,* Text from Book 18, Chapter 3.

Old Testament Messianic Prophecy: The following points of prophecy in the Old Testament confirm Jesus's role as the "anointed one."

The Messiah would be born in Bethlehem. (Micah 5:2)

The Messiah would be born in the line of Jacob. (Genesis 35:10–12)

The Messiah would be born of the tribe of Judah. (Genesis 49:10)

The Messiah would be of the house of David. (2 Samuel 7:12–16)

The Messiah would perform many miracles. (Isaiah 35:5–6)

The Messiah would speak in parables. (Psalm 78:2)

The Messiah would be rejected by His own people. (Isaiah 8:14)

The Messiah would come while the temple stands. (Malachi 3:1)

The Messiah would be betrayed for thirty pieces of silver. (Zechariah 11:12)

The Messiah would be resurrected from the dead. (Psalm 16:10)

These are only a few of the Old Testament prophecies that were fulfilled in the life, death, and resurrection of Jesus of Nazareth.

The Probabilities: Taking these Scriptures into account, what is the probability that Jesus was the actual Messiah described in the prophetic writings of the Old Testament? In his thought provoking series known as the *Case for Christ,* an investigative journalist named Lee Strobel examined the evidence concerning Jesus. As a self-professed atheist, Strobel completed an extensive investigation of the evidence surrounding the case for Jesus as the prophesied Messiah. In this fascinating work, Strobel uncovered the following data: "A college professor of mathematics and astronomy named Dr. Peter Stoner wanted to determine what the odds were that any human being throughout human history could have fulfilled the messianic prophecies. In his study entitled "Science Speaks," Stoner presented his findings—estimating that the odds of any single human being fulfilling 48 of these ancient prophecies would be one chance in a trillion, trillion, trillion, trillion, trillion, trillion, trillion, trillion, trillion, trillion, trillion, trillion."[8]

Our Debt Is Paid: When Jesus came to fulfill the role of Messiah, his blood sacrifice on the cross offered forgiveness for those who believed Him to be the Son of God. The apostle Paul explained, "When you were dead in your sins and in the uncircumcision of the flesh, God made you alive with Christ. He forgave us all of our sins, having canceled the charge of our legal indebtedness, which stood against us and condemned us; he has taken it away, nailing it to the cross" (Colossians 2:13–14).

Temple Sacrifice Obsolete: The ultimate sacrifice of Jesus (who had no sin) was given by God the Father in order to reverse the damage done to humankind by Adam. The author of Hebrews wrote, "Unlike the other high priests, he [Jesus] does not need to offer sacrifices day after day, first for his own sins, and then for the sins of the people. He sacrificed for their sins once for all when he offered himself" (Hebrews 7:27).

Understand It

The best evidence that speaks to whether or not Jesus came to fulfill the role of Messiah is the Old Testament prophecies themselves. While some of the writings point to deliberate behavior on the part of Jesus, most of them describe facts that were beyond His control. For instance, how could the Old Testament prophet Zechariah possibly know that, more than five hundred years later, Jesus would be betrayed for thirty pieces of silver?

Instead of continuing the practice of ritual sacrifices at the temple, believers need only accept the one-time and final sacrifice of Jesus as the means of atonement for all their sins. Since Jesus did this work on the cross, the sins of believers have effectively been canceled. The bottom line is this: Jesus

---

[8] Stroebel, 183.

did the heavy lifting, but we reap all the benefits of His efforts. Addiction specialist Dr. Gerald May agrees. "Jesus was the New Adam, the profound love gift of God entering the world to effect a reconciliation of humanity with God … He came for sinners who missed the mark of responding to God's love. To put it bluntly, God became incarnate to save the addicted, and that includes all of us."[9]

Think About It

1. Did you know so many copies of the Bible have survived nearly two thousand years? Why is it important that the versions scholars have found from antiquity are almost entirely identical in terms of content?

2. Why does it matter that there are a number of first-century sources offering corroborating third-party evidence of the details on the life and death of Jesus?

3. Of all the prophecies mentioned, which do you find the most important in terms of validating what the Bible says about Jesus's role as the Messiah?

---

[9] Gerald G. May, *Addiction & Grace* (New York, NY: HarperCollins Publishers, 1988), 115.

Pray About It

As you take time to pray between lessons, here are a few ideas to get you started:

- Ask God to help you understand that your debt has been paid by Jesus on the cross.
- Pray that you fully comprehend the importance of the redemption process that began many thousands of years ago for the benefit of all human beings.
- Thank God that we no longer have to live under the sacrificial laws of Moses to attain forgiveness of our plentiful personal sins.

LESSON 7

JESUS AND FREEDOM

It is not the healthy who need a doctor, but the sick. I have not come to call the righteous, but sinners to repentance.

—**Luke 5:31**

When most people think of the concept of repentance, they imagine tearful admissions and heart-wrenching apologies. But the Bible's idea of what it means to repent is actually much simpler. While it does involve a confession of sorts, it primarily describes a process by which we transform our thoughts and actions entirely.

The New Testament (which literally means "new covenant") was written primarily in Greek. So it is often helpful to look at the original Greek words used in the Gospels to clarify the meanings of important passages. In Greek, the word used for "repent" means "a complete and total change of mind." This definition indicates that, in order to truly repent, we must deliberately turn away from our old way of life and strive to follow a new path.

Jesus often taught important life principles within the subtle mechanisms of a parable. This term (derived from the Greek word *parabole*) means to "lay alongside." So, a parable is a simple story told to illustrate a specific principle by laying alongside the real meaning. Jesus used such stories to explain His teachings in ways that the average follower could understand.

In this case, Jesus used the parable of the prodigal son to illustrate the critical principle of repentance.

Read It

In preparation for this lesson, read the following Scripture: Luke chapter 15.

Study It

The Prodigal Son: In this parable, a prosperous man was the father of two sons. Although it was customary for a father's estate to be divided after his death, the younger son in this story asked for his share of the inheritance during his father's lifetime. This was a bold request to make because the firstborn son in antiquity would have precedence in any division of a father's estate by birthright. It would have been a shameful demand for any son to have made and would have disgraced the family in the surrounding community.

Wild Living: Nevertheless, Jesus explained that the father granted this unusual request and divided his property between his two sons. The younger son then set off for a distant country where he wasted his new-found wealth. "Not long after that, the younger son got together all he had, set off for a distant country and there squandered his wealth in wild living" (Luke 15:13).

Famine Strikes: A severe famine then overtook that distant country, and the son experienced hunger and despair. He eventually hired himself out as a servant to a citizen of the land in order to survive. While working there, he was greatly humbled and forced to feed pigs in the fields. Remember that such an act would have been a major disgrace for any Jew because the Bible forbade Jews from owning, eating, or even being in the presence of pigs. According to Scripture, "He longed to fill his stomach with the pods that the pigs were eating, but no one gave him anything" (Luke 15:16).

Amazing Grace Addiction Bible Study

The Freedom Road: At some point, the younger son's circumstances became so desperate that he longed to return to his father's household—not with the elevated status of a son but as a humble servant. "When he came to his senses, he said, 'How many of my father's hired servants have food to spare, and here I am starving to death! I will set out and go back to my father and say to him: Father, I have sinned against heaven and against you. I am no longer worthy to be called your son; make me like one of your hired servants.' So he got up and went to his father" (Luke 15:17–20).

The Reception: As he approached his home, his father saw him and was overjoyed. "But while he was still a long way off, his father saw him and was filled with compassion; he ran to his son, threw his arms around him and kissed him" (Luke 15:20).

The Celebration: The son confessed his sins, and the father received him with open arms. "The father said to his servants, 'Quick! Bring the best robe and put it on him. Put a ring on his finger and sandals on his feet. Bring the fattened calf and kill it. Let's have a feast and celebrate. For this son of mine was dead and is alive again; he was lost and is found'" (Luke 15:22–24).

Father and Son: Jesus intended for the younger son to be a character to which we could all relate. We have all been guilty of disgracing our heavenly Father by placing our personal desires and cravings above all else. As substance abusers, we have been especially bold in doing so.

God is very much like the father in this story because He loves each of us as children—His children. In fact, God doesn't just *love* us—He's *in love* with us. The Father has been with us always, for better or for worse. As such, God stands by us at all times, even when we choose to worship ourselves and harmful substances instead of Him.

Separation from God: In the story, the son traveled a long distance to a faraway place, creating a great deal of separation between himself and his father. In much the same way, when we act in opposition to the Lord's divine will, we experience spiritual separation from God.

He Came to Himself: The King James Version of Luke 17:15 says of the younger son that "he came to himself." In simple terms, Jesus was saying that the son recognized his sins and realized what he had become. He then reconsidered his position, deciding to turn away from his old life and turn toward home. The son realized he could no longer continue his wild ways, and he began the journey back toward his father and redemption. He made the humbling personal choice to turn away from his sins and return to his father, which is the essence of repentance.

Understand It

Here's the best news of all: we never have to worry about traveling the road home alone. The father in the parable, knowing that his son wanted to return home, was willing to meet him along the way. This same spiritual courtesy is offered to each of us. When we are "still a long way off," God the Father will meet us on the road with a loving, passionate embrace.

Fortunately, we do not have to finish the journey or make the accompanying transformation alone because God will take each step with us and provide a scriptural road map as a guide. Most importantly, we don't have to be "fixed" to come back to God. We only need to make a commitment to meet Him along the way.

Furthermore, we will not be punished or made to pay a penalty for our misdeeds upon our return. God will meet us on the road with open arms and demonstrate exuberant joy regardless of the reception we deserve. Then the process of healing our minds, bodies, and souls can truly begin.

Thankfully, God is not like us. His capacity for forgiveness and compassion knows no bounds. He wants nothing more than for us to turn away from our sins and turn toward Him. While we most certainly have at some point been lost, we may just as easily be found in the arms of God. He loves us unconditionally. The road home may be littered with perils and temptations, but arriving at our destination will be well worth the effort.

Think About It

1) Can you relate to the younger son and the situation described in this parable?

2) Have you ever intentionally sought a degree of separation from God, only to wish to return to His side when things went wrong?

3) Does the concept of wild living sound at all familiar? Have you ever "come to yourself" in the midst of a vicious cycle of substance abuse and called out to God?

Pray About It

As you take time to pray between lessons, here are a few ideas to get you started:

- Ask God to reveal the importance of true repentance in the process of fighting addictive behaviors.
- Pray that God will continually show you His love despite your affinity for wild living.
- Thank God that He is willing to meet you on the road home when you make a decision to repent and return to Him.

LESSON 8

THE SIMPLICITY OF SALVATION

Everyone who calls on the name of the Lord will be saved.
—**Romans 10:13**

Now that we understand the importance of repentance as it relates to addiction, we need to consider the next steps in the spiritual process of salvation. Nearly everyone is familiar with the sentiments expressed in the popular passage that follows: "For God so loved the world that he gave his one and only Son, that whoever believes in him shall not perish but have eternal life" (John 3:16).

The very next verse is far less familiar but is no less important in our understanding of God's plan. "For God did not send his Son into the world to condemn the world, but to save the world through him" (John 3:17).

Jesus, who bore the sins of humankind on the cross, was offered by God as the ultimate sacrifice. This final gift of redemption is available to all who faithfully accept Jesus Christ as the Savior of their lives. Obviously, repentance is an essential step in our reconciliation with God. But if we don't actively pursue a relationship with Jesus, His sacrifice is meaningless for us. In order to complete the salvation process and guarantee our positions in God's eternal kingdom, we must trust in Jesus as the Lord of our lives.

Amazing Grace Addiction Bible Study

Read It

In preparation for this lesson, read the following Scripture: Acts chapter 9.

Study It

The apostle Paul, a former persecutor of Christians, is a perfect example of how the process of redemption works. Paul wrote, "Here is a trustworthy saying that deserves full acceptance: Christ Jesus came into the world to save sinners of whom I am the worst. But for that very reason I was shown mercy so that in me, the worst of sinners, Christ Jesus might display this immense patience as an example for those who would believe in him and receive eternal life." (1 Timothy 1:15–16).

Saul of Tarsus: Prior to his Christian conversion, Paul was known by his Hebrew name, Saul of Tarsus. He was a Pharisee, aptly referred to as a "Hebrew of Hebrews," and a well-known member of the Jewish elite. But before he became a Christian, he spent most of his time speaking against the faith. In fact, he enthusiastically persecuted the early followers of Jesus on a grand scale. He even participated in the stoning death of Stephen (the first Christian martyr), as described in the New Testament book of Acts.

The Road to Damascus: One day, Saul (as he was then known) was traveling north from Jerusalem to arrest and persecute some Christians. When he had an overwhelming encounter with the post-resurrected Christ on the road to Damascus, his life changed dramatically. The passage in Acts 9:3–6 states, "As he neared Damascus on his journey, suddenly a light from heaven flashed around him. He fell to the ground and heard a voice say to him, 'Saul, Saul, why do you persecute me?' 'Who are you Lord?' Saul asked. 'I am Jesus, whom you are persecuting,' he replied."

When Saul got up from the ground, he was blind. He was led into the city and was met there by a follower of Jesus named Ananias. "Then Ananias went to the house and entered it. Placing his hands on Saul, he said,

'Brother Saul, the Lord Jesus, who appeared to you on the road as you were coming here—has sent me so that you may see again and be filled with the Holy Spirit.' Immediately, something like scales fell from Saul's eyes, and he could see again. He got up and was baptized, and after taking some food, he regained his strength" (Acts 9:17–19).

Paul's Legacy: After a time of preparation, Saul then took his Roman name, Paul, and began preaching in the synagogues and gathering places proclaiming Jesus as Messiah. Following the call of Christ, he repented of his sins and dedicated his life in service to God by spreading the Bible's message of redemption and sanctification. In the book of Romans, Paul outlined the remarkably simple process of salvation. "If you confess with your mouth, 'Jesus is Lord,' and believe in your heart that God raised him from the dead, you will be saved. For it is with your heart that you believe and are justified, and it is with your mouth that you confess and are saved" (Romans 10:9–10).

Salvation is really that simple. We must decide to put Jesus first in our lives and forsake our prior entanglements with sin.

Being "Born Again": Another story from the gospel of John helps to further our understanding of experiencing a new birth in Christ. In this passage, a Pharisee named Nicodemus met secretly with Jesus just prior to the crucifixion to have questions answered about His teachings. "Jesus declared, 'Very truly I tell you, no one can see the kingdom of God unless they are born again.' 'How can someone be born when they are old?' Nicodemus asked. 'Surely they cannot enter a second time into their mother's womb to be born!' Jesus answered, 'Very truly I tell you, no one can enter the kingdom of God unless they are born of water and the Spirit. Flesh gives birth to flesh, but the Spirit gives birth to spirit'" (John 3:3–6).

Born from Above: The original Greek translation of the term *born again* meant to be "born from above." Jesus was telling Nicodemus that he had to let his stubborn "old self" die and experience a spiritual rebirth of sorts to become bound to the Lord.

Heart of Stone: A similar idea comes from a passage written by the Old Testament prophet Ezekiel. In it God declares, "I will give them [God's people] an undivided heart and put a new spirit in them; I will remove from them their heart of stone and give them a heart of flesh. Then they will follow my decrees and be careful to keep my laws" (Ezekiel 11:19–20).

In this Old Testament passage, God is telling the people of Israel that, in spite of their disloyalty, He will provide them with new hearts and improved, more obedient spirits. In the same way, Christ offers to take away our stubborn, inflexible, addictive desires by removing our own hearts of stone. Our redeemed hearts will then be softened into flesh and become more flexible and open to correction.

New Replaces Old: When we come to accept Jesus as our personal sacrifice for sins, we are given a brand-new nature. In essence, we are *born again* with this new nature, casting aside the old nature we received at birth—the one sullied by sin in the garden of Eden. Our old nature must cease to exist (die) at the time of our Christian conversion, and we must never again allow it to be resurrected. Paul wrote, "For we know that our old self was crucified with him so that the body of sin might be done away with, that we should no longer be slaves to sin—because anyone who has died has been freed from sin" (Romans 6:6–7).

With hearts willing to make changes, we will be able to set aside our addictions and sinful preoccupations with drugs and alcohol.

Let Go of the Past: Christians are no longer held responsible for the original sin besetting humankind. With the help of Christ, we are given a new spirit to help us fight the battle with our sinful shortcomings. Again, Paul explains, "You were taught with regard to your former way of life, to put off your old self, which is being corrupted by its deceitful desires; to be made new in the attitude of your minds; and to put on the new self, created to be like God in true righteousness and holiness" (Ephesians 4:22–24).

You need to put the reality of your old behaviors in the rear view mirror of life, and let go of the accompanying guilt. You cannot go back and repair all that has been broken, but you can commit to making a change in your body and spirit as you move forward. Drop the burdens of your past by the roadside as you continue your journey, racing with enthusiasm and hope toward the finish line of freedom!

Understand It

Remember that the mistakes you've made in life actually qualify you to be a Christian. If you never sinned, you wouldn't need Jesus. You can't go back and fix all the mistakes you've made, but you can look ahead and not make them again. You have to release your firm grip on the baggage of your past. Having done so, the path ahead becomes free of a major obstacle preventing personal growth and success. God will forgive you; you now need to forgive yourself!

If you have not done so, I urge you to seize this opportunity to accept salvation through Jesus. You have nothing to lose except your former destructive lifestyle. If you wish to continue worshiping drugs and alcohol as your gods, then I would suggest that you do not embrace God's plan. When you are truly born again, you'll become more interested in pleasing God than pleasing yourself.

Think About It

1) Why is Paul's education and personal history important in any discussion about the impact of his writings?

2) What does Paul say that we must do to experience salvation in Romans chapter 10? Have you done this yet? If not, a simple prayer of salvation has been provided at the end of this book to guide you.

3) How can the idea of casting aside our "old nature" in favor of a new, more spiritual nature be useful in gaining a better understanding of how to achieve sustained sobriety?

Pray About It

As you take time to pray between lessons, here are a few ideas to get you started:

- Ask God to reveal the importance of being born again in relation to your everyday battles against addictive behaviors.
- Pray that God will help you to change your old "heart of stone" into a new heart that is more flexible and willing to obey.
- Thank God for helping you let go of your past mistakes so that you can truly move forward in your relationships with Him and others.

UNIT 3

I Once Was Lost, But Now I am Found …
Recognizing the Relationship
between the Holy Spirit and Sin

LESSON 9

THE HOLY SPIRIT

Now the Lord is the Spirit, and where the Spirit of the Lord is, there is freedom.

—2 Corinthians 3:17

As we study the Bible, we must begin to understand the emphasis placed on each member of the Holy Trinity. For the most part, the works of God the Father are emphasized in the stories and language of the Old Testament. We learned how the universe was created, and we learned that God has loved and nurtured us throughout the history of humankind.

The works of Jesus are especially emphasized in the Gospels at the beginning of the New Testament. We learned how Jesus was born, who he was, and how he gave His life for the forgiveness of sins. Although the Gospels tell His story in somewhat different ways, their overall message is consistent. Jesus is God's divine "deliverer," offered to save us all from our sinful selves.

Beginning with the book of Acts, the remainder of the New Testament primary describes the workings of the Holy Spirit. The reality and power of the Spirit of God are proclaimed with emphasis in these remaining books. We will now examine this entity in greater detail to identify its primary purpose in the lives of Christians.

Read It

In preparation for this lesson, read the following Scripture: Acts chapter 2.

Study It

The Holy Trinity: God the Father, Jesus the Son, and the Holy Spirit of God.

God the Father: The works of God the Father are emphasized in the stories and language of the Old Testament. He created the universe and controls everything within it.

Jesus the Son: The works of Jesus are especially emphasized in the Gospels at the beginning of the New Testament. Jesus (the Son) lived in the flesh on the earth as a human being who became the sacrificial offering for our sins.

The Holy Spirit: According to Scripture, the Holy Spirit is a separate entity altogether and is endowed with the divine qualities of both the Father and the Son.

A Watery Illustration: The Holy Trinity has been described in comparison with the natural states of water: as a liquid in its natural form (God), a solid in its more material form (Jesus), and as a gas, like water vapor, in its most effervescent form (the Holy Spirit).

The Spirit Foretold: Jesus introduced His disciples to the concept of the Holy Spirit in speaking to them before his crucifixion. "And I will ask the Father, and He will give you another advocate to help you and be with you forever—the Spirit of truth. The world cannot accept him, because it neither sees him or knows him. But you know him, for he lives with you and will be in you" (John 14:16–17).

Jesus offered these words to tell us that the Holy Spirit would not be visible but would take up residence within the hearts of believers. He continued, "But I tell you the truth, it is for your good that I am going away. Unless I go away, the Advocate will not come to you; but if I go, I will send him to you. When he comes, he will prove [convict] the world to be wrong about sin and righteousness and judgment" (John 16:7–8).

Spirit of Truth: With those words, Jesus tells us that one of the most important functions of the Spirit would lie in its ability to convict us of sin in our lives. Finally, Jesus stated, "But when he, the Spirit of truth comes, he will guide you in all the truth. He will not speak on his own; he will only speak what he hears, and he will tell you what is yet to come. He will glorify me because it is from me that he will receive what he will make known to you" (John 16:13–14).

Instructions: Jesus also spoke the following words to His disciples after the resurrection, just before He ascended to heaven. "Do not leave Jerusalem, but wait for the gift my Father promised, which you have heard me speak about. For John baptized with water, but in a few days you will be baptized with the Holy Spirit ... But you will receive power when the Holy Spirit comes on you; and you will be my witnesses in Jerusalem, and in all Judea and Samaria, and to the ends of the earth" (Acts 1:4–5; 7–8).

A Violent Wind: The apostles (from the Greek word meaning "messengers") obeyed Jesus and stayed in Jerusalem after the ascension. They were still fearful of the Jewish and Roman authorities, so they met secretly, out of the public eye. They gathered with 120 other followers in an upper room fifty days or so after the resurrection to pray and await direction from the Lord. "Suddenly a sound like the blowing of a violent wind came from heaven and filled the whole house where they were sitting. They saw what seemed to be tongues of fire that separated and came to rest on each of them. All of them were filled with the Holy Spirit and began to speak in other tongues as the Spirit enabled them" (Acts 2:2–4).

The Gospel Message: Scripture says that a large group of "God-fearing Jews" from every nation heard the sounds and gathered together at the scene. Peter preached, "Repent and be baptized every one of you in the name of Jesus Christ for the forgiveness of your sins. And you will receive the gift of the Holy Spirit. The promise is for you and your children who are far off—for all whom the Lord our God will call" (Acts 2:38–39).

Pentecost: The Holy Spirit settled upon the apostles, along with three thousand other converts on that day in an event known as *Pentecost* (which in Greek means "fiftieth"). Although the apostles spoke in their own language, the people who gathered there from other nations heard them speaking in their own native languages. The apostles received the gifts of healing and went forth boldly to proclaim the power and authority of God.

The Divine Paraclete: The Holy Spirit is also known as *the divine Paraclete,* which means "one who walks by our side as our counselor, helper, defender, and guide."

The Holy Spirit is God Himself. (Acts 5:3–4)

>The Holy Spirit is ever present. (Psalm 139:7)
>The Holy Spirit is all powerful. (Luke 1:35)
>The Holy Spirit is all knowing. (1 Corinthians 2:10–11)

The Holy Spirit dwells within us. (1 Corinthians 6:19)

Sin and the Spirit: The single most important function of the Holy Spirit in the context of addiction is that it helps to convict us of our sins. Through the direction of the Spirit, our everyday sins and self-destructive behaviors become more recognizable.

Understand It

When we are born again and are baptized with the presence of the Holy Spirit, we become more aware of our natural character defects They are illuminated as being in opposition to our newfound commitment to conduct our lives in ways that honor God. Consequently, sins (and, by extension, substance abuse) become painful thorns in our sides—one that we no longer wish to endure.

The Holy Spirit also has the power to illuminate our minds. Since it lives inside us, the Spirit can distinguish our dangerous, dark qualities from within. The Spirit will identify these internal imperfections and help us to avoid situations that may test our resolve. Accepting the Holy Spirit is like unleashing an internal vacuum cleaner that seeks out all the dirt in our lives and helps us remove it.

By the power of the Holy Spirit, we recognize the need to alter our behaviors and lifestyles accordingly. This is especially true of sins (like addiction) that we have previously been unable to overcome by our own strength. If you've been unable to bring your behavior under control thus far, I urge you not to refuse spiritual help from the genuine Spirit of the living God.

Think About It

1) Were you aware that Jesus foretold the coming of the Holy Spirit before His death?

2) What is the primary function of the Holy Spirit in the lives of Christian believers?

3) Do you believe in the existence of the Holy Spirit? Have you ever had any specific encounters that support your beliefs? Do you have any sin or darkness that you'd like to have removed?

Pray About It

As you take time to pray between lessons, here are a few ideas to get you started:

- Ask God to open your mind to a deeper understanding of the reality and workings of the Holy Spirit.
- Pray that God will allow you to feel the powerful presence of the Spirit in your everyday life.
- Thank God for providing you the gift of the indwelling presence of the Holy Spirit in your battle against addictive behaviors.

LESSON 10

THE SPIRIT AND SELF-CONTROL

For if you live according to the sinful nature, you will die; but if by the Spirit you put to death the misdeeds of the body, you will live.

—**Romans 8:13**

The idea of turning control of our lives over to an entity like the Holy Spirit can be a frightening proposition indeed. So while you may be familiar with the concept, you're probably terrified at the prospect. Although the Alcoholics Anonymous (AA) doctrine of the "higher power" is a step in the right direction, it isn't specific enough in spiritual terms. Nevertheless, we should be willing to take a moment and realize the eternal value of handing the reins of life over to the genuine Spirit of God.

If you're like most people, you've had little success in controlling your addictions on your own. You've fought this battle for years, spending so much time in secular rehabilitation and counseling that the thought of another attempt seems intolerable. I ask you now to consider accepting the salvation of Jesus so that you may have immediate access to the most underrated spiritual power in the universe.

The Holy Spirit can cleanse you of immoral thoughts and behaviors in an immediate and supernatural way. It can help you seize control of your actions in such a miraculous way that the changes are not even difficult to make. The Holy Spirit, as one of its functions, was given the very key to unlock the stubborn door of addiction! So why not place your trust in the gift that God has granted believers for that specific purpose?

Read It

In preparation for this lesson, read the following Scripture: Galatians chapter 5.

Study It

Piloted by the Spirit: When you become a Christian, the Holy Spirit guides you the same way a harbor pilot guides large ships into ports of call. When a large vessel arrives at the mouth of a harbor, the harbor pilot rides a tugboat out and takes over the helm of the ship. He knows where the channels are treacherous and steers the ship away from danger. Since he knows the depths of the water, he prevents ships from running aground in the imperceptible shallows. In much the same way, the Holy Spirit will take charge of your life and help steer you away from danger and irresponsible choices.

The Fruit of the Spirit: In the following passage, Paul introduces us to the concept of the "fruit of the Spirit." This passage describes the characteristics that believers will exhibit when they allow the Holy Spirit to "pilot" them instead of surrendering to the desires of their flesh. "The acts of the flesh are obvious: sexual immorality; impurity and debauchery; idolatry and witchcraft; hatred, discord, jealousy, fits of rage, selfish ambition, dissensions, factions, and envy; drunkenness, orgies and the like … But the fruit of the Spirit is love, joy, peace, forbearance [patience], kindness, goodness, faithfulness, gentleness and self-control" (Galatians 5:19–23).

Acts of the Flesh: This Scripture is important because it begins by revealing the emotions that ruled us as we were piloted by our old self and governed by the flesh. It's interesting to note that the Greek word translated as "witchcraft" in this passage is *pharmakeia,* which is the root word of the modern term *pharmacy.*

Spiritual Fruits: The second half of the Scripture introduces us to the feelings that we are apt to experience when our wills have become subservient to the will of the Holy Spirit. When our lives are piloted by the Spirit of God, we are more likely to exhibit these divine qualities in abundance. The first eight fruits of the presence of the Spirit are similar in nature. When the Holy Spirit takes charge of your life, you'll undoubtedly be a kinder, more loving, compassionate person.

Self-Control: The final fruit of the Spirit on the list is self-control. One cannot overstate the importance of self-control in avoiding a vicious cycle of substance abuse. The word used in the original Greek translation means "to be strong, to control one's thoughts and actions." In basic terms, the presence of the Holy Spirit has been granted to believers so that they can supercharge their ability to muster greater confidence and self-control.

A Spiritual Earpiece: The all-powerful Spirit of God will fight alongside you in the ongoing war against substance abuse. Amazingly, that voice inside you will be the actual voice of God. In her book entitled *Is That You God?* Priscilla Shirer likens this voice to something you have probably seen before. "All Christ's followers are equipped with a powerful tool that attunes our spiritual ears to the Lord's voice. The Holy Spirit is like an IFB—the tiny device news anchors wear in their ears so that their producers can guide their interviews and give them tips on how better to play to the camera."[10]

This is a wonderful illustration of how the Holy Spirit communicates God's will. Instead of hearing a producer, however, we are granted direct access to the thoughts and guidance of the genuine Spirit of God. The Spirit cannot be seen but will offer advice on how to make better choices and live in righteous obedience to God.

---

[10] Priscilla Shirer, *Is That You God?* (Nashville, TN: Lifeway Press, 2009), 44

The Holy Spirit and Addiction: Generally speaking, when the *thought* of abusing chemicals enters our mind, we often allow the *action of using* to immediately follow. The action phase of substance abuse involves taking the steps necessary to acquire the substances, prepare them for use, and ingest them. However, this action phase does not always follow the thought instantaneously, which offers us the opportunity to change our minds and resist the urge to use.

Thoughts vs. Actions: In other words, when we are in the midst of a savage cycle of substance abuse, there is often very little separation between the thought and the action. Even though the thought of using a substance may spark the mechanism of a craving, it does not have the power to necessitate an active response. You may be unable at this point to control your thoughts regarding substances, but you most certainly can control the choice to initiate the action of using.

The Wedge of Choice: The best way to stifle the pangs of temptation is to separate the thought as far as possible from the action. Recognizing these two distinct phases will help you put needed space between them. This space has been occupied by your natural capacity for choice and free will. This wedge of choice is the only thing standing between your desire for substances and your intention to abuse them.

Fill the Gap: Most of us have found that our personal wedge is not strong enough to block the movement from the thought to the action phase. Either we deliberately consider the choice or we blindly proceed to the action phase in our search for an altered state of consciousness. This is precisely the point at which the power and presence of the Holy Spirit needs to be interjected. Paul wrote, "Those who live according to the flesh have their minds set on what the flesh desires; but those who live in accordance with the Spirit have their minds set on what the Spirit desires. The mind governed by the flesh is death, but the mind governed by the Spirit is life and peace" (Romans 8:5–6).

Understand It

We need to attempt to fill the gap between the thought phase of our addiction and the action phase with insight from the Spirit of God. When thoughts or cravings present themselves, we should take a moment to listen to the encouragement and guidance of the Holy Spirit. The Spirit that dwells within us will never instruct us to do anything that is contrary to the will of God.

Remember back to the story of the Hebrews' exit from Egypt found in the second book of the Old Testament. We learned that Moses and the people had been driven to the edge of the Red Sea and trapped there by Pharoah's army. They had no obvious means of escape; only divine intervention could save them. Just before God miraculously parted the waters, Moses told the people the following: "Do not be afraid. Stand firm and you will see the deliverance the Lord will bring you … The Lord will fight for you; you need only to be still" (Exodus 14:13–14).

These words, spoken thousands of years ago, still ring with truth today. If you'll take the time to consider your choices and listen to the guidance of the Holy Spirit, God will fight the battle of addiction on your behalf! The Spirit of God will join you in the battle against cravings, helping you to be victorious in the war against all harmful substances.

Think About It

1) Do you believe that the Holy Spirit has the power to cleanse you of addictive behaviors?

2) Do you agree with the assertion that substance abuse involves the manifestation of both a thought and an action phase?

3) How can we make use of the presence of the Holy Spirit to interrupt our habitual patterns and to fight the battle against addictive behaviors on our behalf?

Pray About It

As you take time to pray between lessons, here are a few ideas to get you started:

- Ask God to grant you greater self-control as described in the fruits of the Spirit.
- Pray that God will give you the strength to begin to separate the thoughts and the actions of abusing intoxicating chemicals.
- Thank God that the Holy Spirit can serve as a wedge of choice in your day-to-day fight against addiction.

LESSON 11

FAITH AND DELIVERANCE

Truly I tell you, if you have faith as small as a mustard seed, you can say to this mountain, "Move from here to there," and it will move. Nothing will be impossible for you.

—**Matthew 17:20–21**

Most people are reluctant to be labeled "addicts" even though their behavior probably merits the title. It's like being made to wear a brightly colored T-shirt that says on the front, "I'm an addict!" And on the back, "I don't deserve your respect." But if you consider the truths of Scripture, you'll realize that as a so-called "addict," you are just being the sinner you were born to be. In order to make a worthwhile change, you need to accept the transforming, redemptive power of Christ and become someone entirely different—a sinner saved by grace.

The biblical definition of grace is simple yet astonishing. The word translated from the original Greek literally means "free gift." So in terms of the Bible, we receive the blessings and favor of God even though we've done absolutely nothing to deserve them. We cannot earn grace. We simply have to accept it as an unmerited gift. As Paul wrote, "For the grace of God has appeared that offers salvation to all people. It teaches us to say 'No' to ungodliness and worldly passions, and to live self-controlled, upright and godly lives in this present age" (Titus 2:11–12).

According to these words from Paul, grace can teach us to lay aside our sins and earthly passions, including intoxicating substances. Some versions of the Bible use the phrase "deliverance from sin" in reference to these verses. In Greek, the word *deliverance* means "salvation." The biblical use of this term means a "freedom from restraint or captivity." Simply put, deliverance is the immediate and miraculous freedom from sin.

Read It

In preparation for this lesson, read the following Scripture: Mark chapter 5.

Study It

Faith Defined: The writer of the book of Hebrews gives us a definition of faith. "Now faith is confidence in what we hope for and assurance about what we do not see" (Hebrews 11:1).

Confidence: The Greek word used in this context for confidence literally means "boldness." This indicates a willingness to ask without fear or hesitation for certain gifts or favors from God. Jesus told His followers, "You may ask me for anything in my name, and I will do it" (John 14:14).

Assurance: The Greek word used here means "certainty." So, the second part of the definition of faith confirms that God is real and provides for us despite the fact that we cannot literally see Him.

Faith and Prayer: Faith is an essential ingredient in a productive life of prayer. Faith allows us to humbly approach God and have confident assurance that our prayers will be answered. Jesus stated quite clearly, "Therefore I tell you, whatever you ask for in prayer, believe that you have received it, and it will be yours" (Mark 11:24).

Amazing Grace Addiction Bible Study

Indiana Jones: When I think of the concept of faith, I am reminded of a particular scene in a popular movie from the 1980s. In the film, "Indiana Jones and the Last Crusade," the title character was on a quest to find the Holy Grail, which was believed to have been the cup used by Jesus at the Last Supper. As the movie reached its climax, Dr. Jones was presented with a daunting test. He found himself on the edge of a large ravine that he needed to cross in order to reach the room containing the holy relic. However, the leap appeared impossible to accomplish through his physical abilities alone.

Nevertheless, Dr. Jones made the decision to close his eyes and step out into the void, based on the premise and the promise of faith. Stepping forward, his foot landed on solid ground in the form of an invisible bridge. This span was imperceptible to the human eye, but it had existed across the divide all along. He wasn't aware of its existence until he stepped out in faith, risked everything, and trusted in God to provide a solution to the problem.

The Bridge of Faith: Fortunately, God has already provided a *bridge* to enable us to avoid a fall, but we must be willing to step out in faith and trust that it will support our weight. This imperceptible span that God created for us has been there all along. It can carry us across the void that exists between us and freedom on the other side.

Mission Impossible: If you cultivate your faith, you can be delivered from your addictions in divine and immediate ways. Jesus confirmed that fact, saying, "With man this is impossible, but with God all things are possible" (Matthew 19:26).

Turning to God: The late Dr. Gerald May was a well-known physician and psychiatrist in the addiction industry for more than twenty-five years. Having counseled many patients successfully over the course of his career, Dr. May was no stranger to the concept of divine intervention. "I identified a few people who seemed to have overcome serious addictions to alcohol and other drugs, and I asked them what had helped them turn their lives around so dramatically ... They kindly acknowledged their appreciation for the professional help they had received, but they also made it clear that this help had not been the source of their healing. What had healed them was something spiritual. It had something to do with turning to God."[11]

Deliverance: Over the years, Dr. May witnessed many real-world examples of these permanent, miraculous healings. "I can only call it deliverance. There is no physical, psychological, or social explanation for such hidden empowerments. People who have experienced them call them miraculous. In many cases, these people have struggled with their addictions for years. Then suddenly, with no warning, the power of addiction is broken."[12]

Deliverance in the Bible: Mark recorded an incident in his gospel that speaks on the subject of deliverance in an interesting way. In this instance, Jesus was traveling early in His ministry with His disciples near the Sea of Galilee. As He approached the shore, a large crowd began to follow Him. "And a woman was there who had been subject to bleeding for twelve years. She had suffered a great deal under the care of many doctors and had spent all she had, yet instead of getting better she grew worse" (Mark 5:25–26).

This woman probably suffered from some type of menstrual disorder. The story continues: "When she heard about Jesus, she came up behind him in the crowd and touched his cloak, because she thought, 'If I just touch his clothes, I will be healed.' Immediately her bleeding stopped and she felt in her body that she was free from her suffering" (Mark 5:27–29).

The Healing Power of Christ: When this woman touched His garment, Jesus realized that "power" had been drawn from Him. He then asked His disciples who had touched Him. The disciples thought this was a strange question because the people in the crowd were pressing against Him on all sides. "Then the woman, knowing what had happened to her, came and fell at his feet and, trembling with fear, told him the whole truth. He [Jesus] said to her, 'Daughter, your faith has healed you. Go in peace and be freed from your suffering'" (Mark 5:33–34).

---

[11] May, 6–7.
[12] May, 153.

Wretched Existence: First of all, we need to understand the gravity of the woman's situation. The Bible says that she suffered such bleeding for twelve years. She must have had a wretched existence but not just because of her health issues. The law of Moses (given in the Old Testament Book of Leviticus) stated that no Jew was allowed to have any contact with a woman suffering from extensive blood loss. She would have been shunned by everyone around her in order that they might keep from becoming ceremonially unclean.

Helpless and Hopeless: The passage also states that the woman suffered under the care of many doctors, having spent all her resources on false cures. Sound familiar? Over the years, I've known countless people who have been in and out of addiction treatment facilities. They've been fed the principles of disease theory with such regularity that they feel helpless and are often unwilling to make additional attempts at rehabilitation. Many families have been ruined by the financial burden of recovery programs, despite the fact that they have seen little or no improvement in their loved ones' behavior.

"Your Faith Has Healed You": According to Mark, the woman in question exhibited an enviable amount of faith in the restorative powers of Jesus. She felt that if she could only "touch his clothes," she would be healed. Her faith was remarkable, considering the fact that Jesus hadn't yet been identified publicly as the Messiah. He was then simply known as a local Jewish teacher who had miraculous powers. Nevertheless, she had probably heard of His teachings and knew about some of the miracles He had performed in the name of God.

Power Goes Out: The passage states that Jesus felt that "power had gone out from him" when He was touched. He knew that someone had reached out to Him and taken healing power. The disciples probably thought He was delusional when He asked who had touched him, considering the size and proximity of the crowd. Nevertheless, Jesus needed to find the woman to confirm she had been healed and to publicly commend her faith.

The Whole Truth: When the woman realized she was well, she fell at Christ's feet and proceeded to tell Him the "whole truth." Have you ever told Jesus the "whole truth" and confessed all the sin that exists in your life?

Understand It

Are you afraid? Do you think you're not good enough or spiritual enough to warrant God's assistance? Or do you think you don't have enough faith? Remember that fear is the opposite of faith. It is the cat to our dog, the hot to our cold, and eventually, the hell to our heaven. In fact, the late great pastor Kenneth Hagin often said, "Fear is faith in the devil."

The Bible clearly states that God provides us an antidote against the diabolical disease of fear. Paul wrote the following: "For God hath not given us the spirit of fear; but of power, and of love, and of a sound mind" (2 Timothy 1:7 KJV).

Are you afraid of asking God for deliverance from your addictive behaviors because you are concerned that He may not answer your prayers? Or are you simply afraid that God will actually answer your prayers?

Think About It

1) Can you relate to the definition of faith provided by the writer of Hebrews in the New Testament? Does it make sense to you personally?

2) Have you ever taken the time to tell Jesus *the whole truth?*

3) Have you known anyone in your life who has been *delivered* in a spiritual way from addictive behaviors? What was their story? Did it have any impact on you? Have you ever actually asked to be delivered by God?

Pray About It

As you take time to pray between lessons, here are a few ideas to get you started:

- Ask God to strengthen your faith as you prepare yourself for the spiritual battles to come.
- Pray that God offers you a healing miracle with regard to your addictive behaviors.
- Thank God for offering you the opportunity to ask for total and complete deliverance from your addictions.

LESSON 12

FIGHTING THE BATTLE

For the Lord your God is the one who goes with you to fight for you against your enemies to give you victory.

—Deuteronomy 20:4

Assuming you have accepted Jesus and repented of your sins (including but not limited to chemical addictions), one question remains. In the course of your everyday life, how wide is the gap between your Saturday nights and your Sunday mornings? In other words, how large of a gap exists between how you live and how God wishes you to live? If you never spoke a word, would your life reflect the moral, ethical, and spiritual values of Christianity?

Sin and obedience to God are polar opposites. Our tendency toward sin is often discussed in biblical terms as a desire to please the flesh, while the concept of obedience is described in terms of pleasing the Spirit. Our flesh is concerned mostly with the pleasures of this world, while the Holy Spirit within us focuses our attention on the principles of integrity and obedience. These two are in a constant tug-of-war for dominance over us. Which one controls your life?

Read It

In preparation for this lesson, read the following Scripture: 1 Corinthians chapter 10.

Study It

You Are God's Temple: The bodies of believers have become the literal dwelling places of God. "Do you not know that your bodies are temples of the Holy Spirit, who is in you, whom you have received from God? You are not your own; you were bought at a price. Therefore honor God with your bodies" (1 Corinthians 6:19–20).

Flesh vs. Spirit: Our flesh is concerned mostly with the pleasures and temptations of this world, while the Holy Spirit within us focuses his attention on the principles of righteousness. We need to train ourselves to listen to the Spirit more and the flesh less in order to avoid the potential for godly correction down the road.

Crank Up the Volume: In fact, the more you listen to and obey the Spirit of God, the less likely you will be to hear and respond to the discord of the Devil. The apostle Paul clearly stated, "So I say, walk by the Spirit, and you will not gratify the desires of the flesh. For the flesh desires what is contrary to the Spirit, and the Spirit what is contrary to the flesh. They are in conflict with each other, so that you are not to do whatever you want" (Galatians 5:16–17).

The Spiritual Upgrade: If Jesus has become an integral part of your life, you are not just you anymore. You have been born again and have been granted a new identity as "You, Version 2.0." Paul wrote, "Therefore, I urge you, brothers and sisters, in view of God's mercy, to offer your bodies as a living sacrifice, holy and pleasing to God—this is your true and proper worship. Do not conform to the pattern of this world, but be transformed by the renewing of your mind. Then you will be able to test and approve what God's will is—his good, pleasing and perfect will" (Romans 12:1–2).

Dealing with Cravings: In the same way that God has authority over the Devil, believers have authority over drugs and alcohol. Addiction specialist Dr Harold Urschel writes, "If you continually resist the urge to drink or use when exposed to a trigger, your body and the hippocampal system in your brain will come to understand that the trigger is not a sign of good things to come. The dopamine system will no longer be automatically activated and eventually the trigger will fail to produce a craving. That's why cravings become weaker the longer you stay sober."[13]

Cravings are nothing more than echoes in your mind. You hear them loud and clear the first few times, but they quickly fade in terms of volume and intensity. If you can establish authority over cravings and attempt to bring your thoughts under control, you will have the ammunition necessary to win each battle and ultimately the war as a whole.

A Bad Neighborhood: Creating more space and time between the actual cravings for alcohol or drugs will provide more of an opportunity to insert the wedge of the Holy Spirit. Listen intently for the voice of the Spirit, as it will never prompt you to behave in any way that is contrary to the will of God the Father. The following words are true in any context: "Your mind is like a bad neighborhood—don't go there alone!"

Temptation: The word *temptation* in the Greek is *peirasmos,* which means a "test or trial." These tests do not come directly from God because he is already aware of the spiritual condition of our hearts and minds. Trials are undoubtedly placed in our paths so that we may discover our true capabilities as believers.

You Are the Tempter: James (the brother of Jesus) wrote, "When tempted, no one should say, 'God is tempting me.' For God cannot be tempted by

---

[13] Harold C. Urschell, III, *Healing the Addicted Brain* (Naperville, IL: Sourcebooks, Inc., 2009), 60.

evil, nor does he tempt anyone; but each one is tempted when by his own evil desire he is dragged away and enticed" (James 1:13).

We alone are responsible for the quality of our own choices, and addiction is a disorder of choice. As so-called addicts, we need to learn to trust in Jesus for the help we need in controlling our deliberate, sinful, addictive behaviors.

Jesus was Tempted: If you recall the discussion on Jesus's preparation to begin His public ministry, He was tempted for forty straight days in the wilderness. He rebuked the Devil three consecutive times with Scripture, and Satan eventually fled. Jesus was tempted directly by the Devil and passed the test with flying colors. It is for this very reason that we may trust in Him to strengthen us during times of trouble. "Because he [Jesus] himself suffered when he was tempted, he is able to help those who are being tempted" (Hebrews 2:18).

Tug-of-War: We need to actively discourage our fleshly thoughts and set our minds on the things of God. Paul instructed the churchgoers at Philippi, "Brothers and sisters, whatever is true, whatever is noble, whatever is right, whatever is pure, whatever is lovely, whatever is admirable—if anything is excellent or praiseworthy—think about such things" (Philippians 4:8).

The daily battle against addiction and sin is nothing more than a spiritual tug-of-war. Unfortunately, our *old self* often presents a problem because it maintains a firm grasp on the rope. While trying to gain proprietorship of our souls, it will pull and tug on that rope until it comes to the realization that the Spirit cannot be defeated.

The War of the Mind: Paul told the church at Corinth that believers are fighting a war in their minds for control of their innermost thoughts and desires. "The weapons we fight with are not the weapons of the world. On the contrary, they have divine power to demolish strongholds. We demolish arguments and every pretension that sets itself up against the knowledge of God, and we take captive every thought to make it obedient to Christ" (2 Corinthians 10:4–5).

Strongholds: Addiction is nothing more than a spiritual stronghold that the Devil and his cohorts will aggressively defend. We must commit to attacking this emotional fortress with all of our might, taking captive our thoughts to make them obedient to Christ. God wants us to be free, and He will help us each and every day to win this battle against substance abuse on both the physical and metaphysical levels.

A Way Out: There is one final point on the subject of strongholds that you need to understand. In spite of the nature of your current situation, the Lord will never give you more temptation than you can handle. Paul wrote, "No temptation has overtaken you except what is common to mankind. And God is faithful; he will not let you be tempted beyond what you can bear. But when you are tempted, he will also provide a way out so that you can endure it" (1 Corinthians 10:13).

Understand It

These are some of the most important passages in the New Testament relating to addictive behaviors. They encourage us to fight the battle for our very own souls by embracing the divine powers granted us as believers in God. As Christians, we are fully capable of demolishing the stubborn strongholds of our addictions and persistent preoccupations with intoxicating chemicals. If we can learn to change our states of mind and redirect our thoughts in ways that promote responsible choices, we can break free from the captivity of substance abuse and experience the freedom of sustained sobriety.

In the final passage, Paul said that you will face temptations every day that are not uncommon to others. He stressed that God is ever faithful and will never allow you to be tempted beyond your capacity to withstand. If you plan on memorizing any Scripture to aid you in battle, consider making it this one (1 Corinthians 10:13). When you are in the midst of a seemingly impossible cycle of provocations, remember that God will always provide a means of escape!

Think About It

1. Can you relate to the discussion about obeying the desires of the flesh versus those of the Spirit? If cravings become less frequent when they are ignored over time, how important is it in your recovery to block them out and focus only on the voice of the Holy Spirit?

2. Do you agree with the biblical definition for the word *temptation?* Have you ever viewed a craving in the context of a test or trial? Do you understand that no matter how much temptation you face, God will always offer you a means of escape?

3. Do you understand that, as a believer, your body is literally the temple of the Holy Spirit? Have you been treating it that way?

Pray About It

As you take time to pray between lessons, here are a few ideas to get you started:

- Ask God to help you "take captive every thought" that relates to addiction and substance abuse.
- Pray that God helps you understand that you can establish authority over your persistent cravings for intoxicating chemicals.
- Thank God for offering divine assistance in the spiritual tug-of-war between the flesh and the Spirit.

UNIT 4

I Was Blind, but Now I See!
Winning the Spiritual Battle Against
the Devil and Sin

LESSON 13

THE ENEMY

Be alert and of sober mind. Your enemy the devil prowls around like a roaring lion looking for someone to devour.

—1 Peter 5:8

According to recent public surveys, more than 90 percent of Americans believe in God. But according to the very same polls, only 57 percent of Americans believe in the Devil.[14] This is a curious discrepancy, considering the sinister nature of the world around us. Why is this so?

Perhaps it's because it seems to be in our nature as human beings to dwell on the good rather than the bad. This can be problematic because life doesn't always end in "happily ever after." In reality, disharmony in life is the rule rather than the exception, and chaos is most often the result. The biblical name for the architect of this chaos and the prince of this fallen world is Satan. The English transliteration of the Hebrew word *Satan* means "adversary," while the Greek word is most often translated as "hostile opponent."

How do you picture the Devil? Perhaps you envision some harmless version of a crimson comic book character holding a pitchfork. This popular image, which has been reinforced on television and in the movies, helps to set our mind at ease and create the illusion that the Devil is a matter

---

[14] http://www.YouGov.com Survey, "Exorcism and the Devil," September 12, 2013.

of folly and not fact. In the minds of many, he dwells alongside fairies, leprechauns, and teenage wizards with magic wands. And that's right where the Devil wants to be—behind the wreckage and firmly out of view. You see, Satan doesn't want us to actually believe in him, but he does want us to follow him.

Read It

In preparation for this lesson, read the following Scripture: Job chapter 1.

Study It

Spiritual Warfare: The Bible is quite clear in stating that angels, demons, and the Devil most certainly exist. For example, the Old Testament book of 2 Kings tells a story about the prophet Elisha. The following events took place when Israel was at war with the king of Aram from Damascus (Syria). In the passage, Elisha was counseling Joram, the Israelite king, during the war and delivering direct instructions from God. As a result, things were not going well for the army of Aram. Their ruthless king reasoned that killing Elisha would turn the tide, and he would win the war against Israel. So he sent a large force of chariots and soldiers to surround the city of Dothan, Elisha's headquarters.

The very next morning, Elisha was awakened by his servant and told that the enemy had arrived during the night and besieged their city. Elisha responded, "'Don't be afraid,' the prophet answered. 'Those who are with us are more than those who are with them.' And Elisha prayed, 'Open his eyes, Lord, so that he may see.' Then the Lord opened the servant's eyes, and he looked and saw the hills full of horses and chariots of fire all around Elisha" (2 Kings 6:16–17).

In this story, the Lord had foreseen Elisha's circumstances and sent an army of angels to his aide. The invading soldiers were then blinded by God and led away from the city, thereby ending their occupation of Israel.

The Spirit Realm Is Real: This account is interesting because it represents the attitude that most people have regarding the reality of the spirit world. The servant's reaction is natural and understandable in any context. When God "opened the servant's eyes," he could see the angelic provisions that had been made for their protection. The Bible provides a thorough description of the ongoing spiritual war that is being waged around us every day, and as believers, we need to accept this reality. You would foolish not to believe in demons and the Devil because they certainly believe in you.

Guardian Angels: Do you believe in guardian angels? Interestingly, the reality of their existence does have a basis in Scripture. "If you say, 'The Lord is my refuge,' and you make the Most High your dwelling, no harm will overtake you, no disaster will come near your tent. For he will command his angels concerning you to guard you in all your ways; they will lift you up in their hands, so that you will not strike your foot against a stone" (Psalm 91:9–12).

If you believe in guardian angels, then you should definitely believe in demons and the Devil!

Who Is Satan? Satan was created by God as a guardian cherub, which is one of the most powerful types of angels. As a member of God's court, his basic duty was to accuse humans before God. "You were the model of perfection, full of wisdom and perfect in beauty ... You were anointed as a guardian cherub, for so I ordained you. You were on the holy mount of God" (Ezekiel 28:12, 14).

Lucifer Rebels: At some point, Lucifer (meaning "son of the morning" in Hebrew) decided that he was not content to simply *serve* God, but that he wanted to be *like* God. "You [Lucifer] said in your heart, 'I will ascend to the heavens; I will raise my throne above the stars of God; I will sit enthroned on the mount of assembly ... I will ascend above the tops of the clouds; I will make myself like the Most High'" (Isaiah 14:13–14).

The Devil saw the power that God possessed and wanted it for himself. So he decided to rebel out of a sense of ego and pride against the God who created him. Not surprisingly, God condemned his selfishness and banished him from heaven. "Your heart became proud on account of your beauty, and you corrupted your wisdom because of your splendor. So I threw you to the earth" (Ezekiel 28:17).

When he departed, Satan convinced a third of the angels in heaven to defect with him. These so-called "fallen angels" make up the spectral corps of demons that serve him today.

The Devil's Mission: Satan's primary goal on this earth is to disparage the name of Jesus and wreak havoc in the lives of men, women, and children. Pastor Chip Ingram explains, "When scripture speaks of Satan, it isn't confined to small, passing comments or figures of speech. Satan is not a metaphor for evil. He is a powerful angel who committed treason against his Creator and convinced a third of the angels to rebel along with him. He now seeks to destroy all that is good and God-ordained, and his strategy ever since his fall has been to tempt us with the same agenda he had—to be like God."[15]

A Created Being: Since Satan is a created being, he has limitations. He is not an all-powerful entity. He cannot read your mind, and he cannot directly control your behavior. He can only observe you and offer temptations that seem consistent with your actions.

Satan vs. Job: It is important to understand that the Devil can do you no harm without the expressed permission of God the Father. This principle is best illustrated in the first chapter of the book of Job. "One day the angels came to present themselves before the Lord, and Satan also came with them. The Lord said to Satan, 'Where have you come from?' Satan answered the Lord, 'From roaming throughout the earth, going back and forth on it.' Then the Lord said to Satan, 'Have you considered my servant Job? There is no one on earth like him; he is blameless and upright, a man who fears God and shuns evil'" (Job 1:6–8).

---

[15] Chip Ingram, *The Invisible War* (Ada, MI: Baker Books, 2007), 47.

Satan Challenges God: Satan believed that Job was only a righteous man because he prospered and received God's favor. So he challenged God to take away all Job's possessions with the intention of getting him to curse the Lord. "The Lord said to Satan, 'Very well, then, everything he has is in your power, but on the man himself do not lay a finger'" (Job 1:12).

Despite the Devil's efforts to destroy him, Job refused to curse God. His faith remained strong throughout his time of testing. As a result of his faithfulness, his family and his fortunes were ultimately restored.

God Is In Charge: Before he could destroy anything in Job's life or even touch a hair on his head, the Devil had to get God's permission. So it's clear that God has authority over Satan at all times. Although the Lord may allow the Devil to tempt us on occasion, He will always keep Satan on a short leash.

Who's to Blame? The Devil cannot be blamed for the flaws in your personal character. Remember that the Devil cannot control your life unless you and God allow him to do so. As stated many times before, you alone control your choices and behavior. A silly excuse like "The Devil made me do it!" has no value in terms of theology or reality.

Victory in Jesus: The good news is that while the Devil has not given up the fight, the victory has already been won by Jesus on the cross. The apostle Paul affirmed this when he wrote, "But thanks be to God! He gives us the victory through our Lord Jesus Christ" (1 Corinthians 15:57).

Understand It

The Devil and his demonic henchmen primarily exist to destroy the lives of Christians and corrupt the name of Christ. The bad news is that they will use any tool (including intoxicating chemicals) at their disposal to achieve that end. Although the Devil's fate was decided by Christ at the cross, he is still launching his final attacks in a futile effort to tempt people to follow his lead. Although Satan knows that he cannot win, he is not yet willing to admit defeat. He'll continue the fight, but ultimately his defeat is inevitable.

On some level, we all know that hallucinogenic substances are modern versions of the forbidden fruit consumed by Adam and Eve in the garden. They are sinfully seductive in nature and offer the promise of godlike aspirations, which mankind has come to crave. They falsely promote the expectation of unlimited pleasure and power but are nothing more than spiritual distractions.

When we ignore the commands of the Lord and "take a bite," the Devil deceives us into believing that this forbidden treat will transform us and our souls into the "gods of independence." In reality, a positive choice to abstain will result in the opposite condition—dependence on God.

Think About It

1. Do you believe the Devil is real? If so, how do you imagine him in your mind? Do you believe in guardian angels?

2. Why does it matter that the Devil is a created being? What difference does this make in terms of his authority?

3. Do you think it's appropriate to blame the Devil for our addictions? Can the Devil make us do things that we do not wish to do?

Pray About It

As you take time to pray between lessons, here are a few ideas to get you started:

- Ask God to open your spiritual eyes so that you may gain a deeper understanding of the spiritual war that rages around you every day.
- Pray that God creates a spiritual hedge of protection around you and your loved ones as you fight the battle against the dark forces of addiction.

- Thank God for sending Jesus on your behalf to win the ultimate and final victory over the Devil on the cross at Calvary.

LESSON 14

WEAPONS OF WAR

Finally, be strong in the Lord and his mighty power. Put on the full armor of God so that you can take your stand against the devil's schemes. For our struggle is not against flesh and blood, but against the rulers, against the authorities, against the powers of this dark world and against the spiritual forces of evil in the heavenly realms.

—Ephesians 6:10

It's important to remember that while the Devil is still fighting the battle, the war has already been won. When Jesus died on the cross, the Devil was defeated—once and for all time. Although his fate has already been decided, Satan is still launching his final attacks in a futile effort to tempt people to follow his lead.

If you have made the decision to give your life to Christ, then you need to understand one very important thing. You have joined the winning team and chosen a position in opposition to Satan and the forces of darkness. As such, you have placed a target on your back and need to be prepared for spiritual warfare on a grand scale.

According to the apostle Paul, to protect yourself in battle, you need to put on the *full armor of God*. The following Scriptures describe the spiritual process by which we can not only defend ourselves from the attacks of the Devil but go on the offensive at times, operating under the power and authority of God the Father. Each piece of this spiritual armor is drawn from the actual equipment used by the typical first century Roman soldier.

Read It

In preparation for this lesson, read the following Scripture: Ephesians chapter 6.

Study It

The Belt of Truth: The first piece of armor is described in the following passage: "Stand firm then, with the belt of truth buckled around your waist ..." (Ephesians 6:14).

This was typically the first piece of armor to be put on by soldiers in antiquity because its sole purpose was to hold together the rest of the protective gear in battle. Paul calls it the "belt of truth" because he indicated that we must be willing to accept the entire truth of salvation in order for it to function properly. In addition, our lives as Christians should be obvious demonstrations of the power and presence of the spiritual truths of God.

The Breastplate of Righteousness: Paul describes the second piece of armor as follows: "Stand firm then, with the belt of truth buckled around your waist, with the breastplate of righteousness in place ..." (Ephesians 6:14–15).

When we have strengthened our resolve by putting on this "breastplate of righteousness," we can rest assured that God will lend His unlimited supernatural power to guard our hearts from harm. The principles of righteousness should guide our paths as Christians and provide useful ammunition in the fight against the dark forces of the Devil.

The Footgear of the Gospel: The third item described by Paul involves the legs and feet. "Stand firm then, with the belt of truth buckled around your waist, with the breastplate of righteousness in place, and with your feet fitted with the readiness that comes from the gospel of peace" (Ephesians 6:14–15).

Paul was indicating we need to prepare our legs and feet for the battle ahead. Soldiers are unable to maneuver effectively in battle without protection for their feet. The "gospel of peace" should serve to provide a firm foundation for our bodies and a mechanism by which we can accomplish the will of God.

The Shield of Faith: The fourth piece of armor is essential for spiritual defense. "In addition to all this, take up the shield of faith, with which you can extinguish all the flaming arrows of the evil one" (Ephesians 6:16).

Roman soldiers typically carried a large, convex shield into battle. The size of the shield was sufficient to provide protection from hostile infantrymen. Leather coverings on the shield would allow the flaming arrows of the enemy to embed themselves in the shield and snuff out the flames. In terms of addiction, the Devil most certainly uses the *flaming arrows* of drugs and alcohol as weapons against us.

The Helmet of Salvation: The fifth item described is mentioned in the following passage: "In addition to all this, take up the shield of faith, with which you can extinguish all the flaming arrows of the evil one. Take the helmet of salvation ..." (Ephesians 6:16-17).

Paul clearly intended for us to understand that protecting our minds from an addictive onslaught would be of primary importance. The rest of the body cannot function if our head suffers a deadly blow in a physical or spiritual conflict. We must keep our minds on our salvation and protect our thoughts from demonic infiltration.

The Sword of the Spirit: The sixth and final piece of spiritual armor described by Paul is perhaps the most important of all. "In addition to all this, take up the shield of faith, with which you can extinguish all the flaming arrows of the evil one. Take the helmet of salvation and the sword of the Spirit, which is the word of God" (Ephesians 6:16-17).

Paul probably intended to present the idea that God's Word—the Holy Scriptures—should be used in spiritual battle, not only for defensive purposes but to strike out offensively against the enemies of darkness. The Word of God can repel any attack and can be used as an offensive weapon to subdue even the most formidable demonic adversaries. The Word of God, as presented in Scripture, can be used to cut Satan and his evil minions to shreds. "For the word of God is alive and active. Sharper than any double-edged sword, it penetrates even to dividing soul and spirit, joints and marrow; it judges the thoughts and attitudes of the heart" (Hebrews 4:12).

The Bottom Line: When the will of Christian believers is in agreement with God's will, the Devil's influence can be resisted. James, the brother of Jesus, wrote, "Submit yourselves, then, to God. Resist the devil, and he will flee from you. Come near to God and he will come near to you" (James 4:7).

Understand It

The most important thing to understand about the reality of spiritual warfare is that you can absolutely win these battles in the name of God. When you are suffering from a physical or spiritual attack related to addiction, you need to learn to wield the Word of God as an offensive weapon to claim a victory over the Devil and his minions. When faithful believers are under attack, they can use Scripture to protect themselves and strike back against the Enemy.

Often people who understand the truly sinister nature of the Enemy will speak certain Scriptures aloud when they are under a significant demonic assault. Remember that the Devil and his demons cannot read your mind. They can only observe you from the outside, so it is important to speak the Scriptures out loud when rebuking Satan in the name of God. You can memorize a few short passages, or simply tell the Devil to depart in the name of Jesus! You can also recite aloud the Lord's Prayer, which is a powerful weapon against the forces of darkness. This may feel a little strange at first, but it is a proven way to fight demonic oppression in the form of substance abuse. "Our Father, who art in heaven, Hallowed by thy name. Thy kingdom come. Thy will be done in earth as it is in heaven. Give us this day our daily bread. And forgive us our debts, as we forgive our debtors. And lead us not into temptation, but deliver us from evil: For Thine is the kingdom, and the power, and the glory, forever. Amen" (Matthew 6:9–13 KJV).

If we resist the Devil and allow the Holy Spirit to help us fight our addictive urges, Satan will flee the scene in a hurry. The Word of God is "sharper than any double-edged sword," and it has the ability to cut directly into the heart of Satan and his dark disciples. God's Word can turn a full-on demonic assault into a frenzied retreat in seconds.

Think About It

1. Can you relate to Paul's discussion on spiritual armor and its importance in fighting the everyday battle against the Devil and his demonic cohorts?

2. Do you understand that we all have targets on our backs when it comes to attracting attention from the Devil, especially if we've ever had a problem with addiction?

3. What are your strengths and weaknesses in terms of spiritual armor? Do you feel prepared to use the sword of the Spirit (the Word of God) in battle?

Pray About It

As you take time to pray between lessons, here are a few ideas to get you started:

- Ask God to help you understand the importance of putting on the spiritual armor of God in fighting battles against the Enemy.
- Pray that God helps you to learn the Bible so that you may make use of His word as an offensive weapon in the fight for sobriety and spiritual peace.

- Thank God for always taking your side in the everyday struggle against addictions and the evil forces that promote them.

LESSON 15

ADDICTION AND OBEDIENCE

Whoever does not take up their cross and follow me is not worthy of me. Whoever finds their life will lose it, and whoever loses their life for my sake will find it.

—**Matthew 10:38–39**

As a so-called "addict," you've been told that you have a crippling, lifelong disease and are unable to control your dependent behaviors. Allegedly, addictive chemicals have the power to eliminate your capacity for free will and turn you into a helpless, hopeless slave. Having been labeled an addict for years, you may eventually come to accept this grim diagnosis as fact. As a result, you begin to give up the fight and feel justified in exhibiting the symptoms of the so-called disease. Understandably, you may start to rationalize your destructive behavior in the context of your new-found sickness. Naturally, you come to accept your fate by thinking, *If I'm going to be treated like an addict, I may as well act like one.* In this way, addiction for many people becomes a self-fulfilling prophecy. The following passage by addiction specialist Dr. Abraham Twerski illustrates this point.

Suppose you had an automobile that was operating well, but a part became defective. You would replace the defective part and the car would run well again. If, however, you found your car was a "lemon" and each time you corrected a problem something else went wrong, you might throw your hands up in disgust. You might justifiably conclude there is no purpose in getting the car repaired. This is what happens in addictive thinking. The profound shame that addicts feel results in their thinking that it is futile to change their ways.[16]

The bottom line is this: the more confidence you have in your ability to break a cycle of addiction, the more successful you can be in doing so. The concept of the "helpless addict" is a troubling misconception that has been spread throughout the field of addiction like the disease it supposedly describes. There is nothing different (physically or genetically) about you that condemns you to a lifetime of struggle.

Read It

In preparation for this lesson, read the following Scripture: Ephesians chapter 4.

Study It

The Great "I Am": How many times have you said the words, "I am an addict" or "I am an alcoholic"? Millions of people have willingly accepted these titles without really understanding their impact in spiritual terms. In the book of Exodus, Moses asked God for His name just before returning to Egypt to demand the release of the Hebrew slaves from the pharaoh. "God said to Moses, 'I AM WHO I AM.' This is what you are to say to the Israelites. 'I AM' has sent me to you" (Exodus 3:14).

Responding to Moses, God called himself the great "I Am!" In addition, Christ spoke those same words seven times in the gospel of John alone in reference to the numerous titles that he embraced: Good Shepherd, Bread of Life, and the way, the truth, and the life. So, when you willingly accept the label of an addict or an alcoholic, you are unintentionally corrupting the very name of God.

---

[16] Abraham J. Twerski,, *Addictive Thinking* (Center City, MN: Hazelden, 1990), 69.

The Problem: The Ten Commandments give us a very specific provision against abusing the name of God. "You shall not misuse the name of the Lord your God, for the Lord will not hold anyone guiltless who misuses his name" (Exodus 20:7).

So, when you surrender your will to addiction and give in by speaking the words, "I am an addict," you are blaspheming the divine name of God. You should never give in and speak such a curse over yourself and your life. You are a literal masterpiece of God, and the Bible affirms this fact. "For we are God's masterpiece. He has created us anew in Christ Jesus, so that we can do the good things he planned for us long ago" (Ephesians 2:10 NLT).

Obedience in the Bible: Let's look back at a moment near the end of the life of Moses when the Israelites were in the midst of their forty year period of wandering in the wilderness. As they awaited instruction from God prior to entering the Promised Land, Moses told the people, "See, I am setting before you today a blessing and a curse—the blessing if you obey the commands of the Lord your God that I am giving you today; the curse if you disobey the commands of the Lord your God and turn from the way that I command you today by following other gods" (Deuteronomy 11:26–28).

God lets you choose between a "blessing and a curse." Ultimately, the choice is yours and yours alone. The path to peace begins and ends with one simple word: obedience. The apostle Peter said it well. "As obedient children, do not conform to the evil desires you had when you lived in ignorance. But just as he who called you is holy, so be holy in all you do" (1 Peter 1:14–15).

The Bottom Line: In terms of addiction, you are faced with one very simple choice: Do you obey chemicals, or so you obey God?

The Excuse of Addiction: Most modern dictionaries agree when it comes to the definition of the word *excuse*. They state quite clearly that this word means nothing more than "an attempt to try to remove blame." Spiritually speaking, many people use the so-called disease of addiction as an excuse to remove blame from themselves for their inappropriate behaviors. When we run out of people to blame for our addictive behaviors, we often try to blame the chemicals themselves.

Waiting for Rock Bottom? The idea that people can wait until they hit "rock bottom" is not only absurd but dangerous. This notion often encourages addicts to continue using drugs or alcohol (or both) until they feel they've reached this metaphorical bottom—one which is only identifiable after the fact. At that point, these people seriously question the value of life, itself. Since many people only recognize their personal bottoms in retrospect, this concept encourages the continuation of self-destructive behaviors until an emotional, relational, or physical decline prevails. Realistically, when you've reached the point where using chemicals is more valuable to you than sobriety and life itself, you've hit rock bottom!

However, God wants to keep you out of this pit and has an entirely different future planned for you physically and spiritually. As Isaiah 38:17–18 states, "Surely it was for my benefit that I suffered such anguish. In your love you kept me from the pit of destruction; you have put all my sins behind your back. For the grave cannot praise you, death cannot sing your praise; those who go down to the pit cannot hope for your faithfulness."

Problems in Living: It is an undeniable fact that many people abuse substances as a means of detaching from the problems of everyday life. Countless substance abusers have horrific personal histories, ranging from physical abuse to sexual molestation. If you have ever suffered similar outrages, those issues need to be addressed. However, you cannot allow such tragic events to assume a position of power in your life, serving as a convenient excuse for destructive behaviors. If you ignore your problems by self-medicating and feeling sorry for yourself, it's time to *stop!*

Habits and Habitat: When you took your first drink or smoked your first joint, were you alone? The answer is probably no, and the majority of addicts will give the same answer. So what makes you think you can remain in that same environment and have any chance at all of changing your behavior? On this subject, Paul wrote the following in his first letter to the church at Corinth. "Do not be misled: 'Bad company corrupts good character'" (1 Corinthians 15:33).

He addressed the issue again in his second letter to the Corinthians. "Do not be yoked together with unbelievers. For what do righteousness and wickedness have in common? Or what fellowship can light have with the darkness?" (2 Corinthians 6:14)

Put on the New Self: Again, the key point to be made involves replacing your corrupt old self with a new creation in Christ. The apostle Paul wrote, "You were taught with regard to your former way of life, to put off your old self, which is being corrupted by its deceitful desires; to be made new in the attitude of your minds; and to put on the new self, created to be like God in true righteousness and holiness" (Ephesians 4:22).

Understand It

People who use alcohol and drugs are often hesitant to make changes (even temporary ones) in their addictive environments. Addicts, like most people, are comfortable in familiar places and around familiar faces. Comfort, however, can be a deceiving emotion because it can mask the reality of addictive situations. If your environment has contributed to your addiction, then you need to let it contribute to your sobriety by changing it.

Who are you, and what do you believe? You choose where you live; you choose the company you keep; you choose how you respond to stress and problems in living, You choose it all! In order to make better choices, you need to make changes in what you believe. When you commit to embracing this *new self* in Christ, you take a significant step toward becoming the person God wants you to be!

Think About It

1. Do you use intoxicating chemicals to self-medicate, or do you simply do it for the experience itself?

2. Have you personally ever used your addiction as an excuse to explain self-destructive behaviors? If so, will you ever do it again?

3. Do you obey the call of chemicals, or do you obey the call of God?

Pray About It

As you take time to pray between lessons, here are a few ideas to get you started:

- Ask God to help remind that you are His masterpiece and to never again allow yourself to be called an addict.
- Pray that God shows you that obedience is a necessary component of living a blessed Christian life.
- Thank God for making you a "new creature" in Christ.

LESSON 16

ADDICTION AND JUDGMENT

For we must all appear before the judgment seat of Christ, so that each of us may receive what is due us for the things done while in the body, whether good or bad.

—2 Corinthians 5:10

If you believe that God exists and that heaven and hell are real, then you should also believe that humankind will be judged at the end of the current age. This is not some abstract idea that comes from an obscure ancient text but a real event that will take place—whether you're ready for it or not. Humankind will be judged for things said and done in life, and the bad news is that our addictions and other sins will be a major topic of discussion.

However, the good news is that as a Christian, you will have Jesus to argue on your behalf. He (who committed no sin) will intercede for you with the Father. He has wiped away your sins and taken the punishment that you deserve. Jesus sacrificed himself for your personal sins and wants nothing more than for you to spend eternity at His side. But in order to receive this divine endorsement and enter the gates of heaven, you must make a conscious, deliberate choice to follow Christ.

Read It

In preparation for this lesson, read the following Scripture: Luke chapter 23.

Study It

Final Judgment: The New Testament book of Revelation gives us a God-inspired account of the events that will come to pass in the last days. The writer of this book (most likely the apostle John) wrote about a vision he experienced concerning the end of the world. "And I saw the dead, great and small, standing before the throne, and books were opened. Another book was opened, which is the book of life. The dead were judged according to what they had done as recorded in the books ... Anyone whose name was not found written in the book of life was thrown into the lake of fire" (Revelation 20:12–15).

The Book of Life: When the time comes, God won't ask whether or not you are prepared to leave this earth; He'll simply make it happen! When He does, the question is will your name be written in the Book of Life?

Christ at the Cross: According to the gospel of Luke, when Jesus was led out to be crucified, He was executed along with two criminals—one on His left and one on His right. As they awaited certain death on the cross, one of these men cried out to Jesus. Luke described the scene. "One of the criminals who hung there hurled insults at him: 'Aren't you the Messiah [Christ]? Save yourself and us!'" (Luke 23:39).

Jesus said nothing, but the other condemned man immediately came to His defense. "But the other criminal rebuked him. 'Don't you fear God,' he said, 'since you are under the same sentence? We are punished justly, for we are getting what our deeds deserve. But this man has done nothing wrong'" (Luke 23:40–41).

Pick a Side: This scene is representative of the situation that all humankind will face as they look death and judgment in the eye. For the purposes of this discussion, I imagine the defiant criminal to be on the left and the penitent man to be on the right. Where do you stand in proximity to Christ—on His left or right?

Right or Left? Heaven or Hell? If you hang to the left, you are not yet ready to admit your faults and accept His forgiveness. You choose disobedience and mockery over healing and deliverance. You've chosen substances over sobriety, yourself over God, and eventually hell over heaven.

If you hang on the right, you have reached a turning point in your life. You recognize your sins and deliberately repent of your colorful past. You realize that Jesus took the punishment that you deserve, and you're ready to be redeemed.

Paradise Awaits: The biblical account continued after the man on the right criticizes the other criminal for his lack of faith and compassion. The penitent criminal then made the following request: "Jesus, remember me when you come into your kingdom" (Luke 23:42).

The story concludes with Jesus speaking some of the most joyful words ever recorded. "Jesus answered him, 'Truly I tell you, today you will be with me in paradise'" (Luke 23:43).

It took only a few seconds for the penitent criminal to ask Jesus for the keys to the kingdom of heaven. The same can be true for you.

Make a Choice: You have the absolute right to make the decision to refuse to follow God. However, if you choose a life of independence over a life dependent on God, you will undoubtedly face the consequences. Jesus said, "Whoever is not with me is against me, and whoever does not gather with me scatters" (Matthew 12:30).

In this life, there are choices to be made: sin or salvation, addiction or sobriety, hell or heaven. I urge you not to wait until it's too late to choose sides. C. S. Lewis wrote, "Never fear. There are only two kinds of people in the end: those who say to God, 'Thy *will* be done,' and those to whom God says, in the end, '*Thy* will be done.' All that are in hell choose it."[17] (Emphasis added).

Remember that hell is more than a destination; it's a choice!

Choose Wisely: Remember that if you choose not to make a decision, you still have made a choice. Like it or not, you will have taken a deliberate stance in opposition to God. The consequences of not recognizing God's authority and/or deciding not to follow Him are one in the same. Paul issued a final, stern warning from God, saying, "He will punish those who do not know God and do not obey the Gospel of our Lord Jesus. They will be punished with everlasting destruction and shut out from the presence of the Lord and from the glory of his might" (2 Thessalonians 1:8–9).

Take a Stand: Where do you stand in relation to God? Have you made your choice? The author of the book of Hebrews wrote, "God again set a certain day, calling it Today … 'Today, if you hear his voice do not harden your hearts'" (Hebrews 4:7).

The Last Word: Jesus made about a dozen appearances to various people in His post-resurrection body. The final and perhaps most important one was on a mountaintop in Galilee where He told his disciples to gather. At that time, He said, "All authority in heaven and on earth has been given to me. Therefore go and make disciples of all nations, baptizing them in the name of the Father and of the Son and of the Holy Spirit, and teaching them to obey everything I have commanded you. And surely I am with you always, to the very end of the age" (Matthew 28:18–20).

Understand It

Make today the most important day of your life by praying a solemn, quiet prayer for salvation in Christ. If you don't know what to say, I

---

[17] C. S. Lewis, *The Great Divorce* (San Francisco, CA: HarperCollins, 1946), 75.

have included a simple prayer at the end of this book. If you've already done so, you have undoubtedly made the most important decision of all. Although life will still be filled with obstacles big and small, you will never again have to navigate them alone. When you find yourself headed into dangerous waters, let the Holy Spirit take the wheel, and your spiritual battle with addiction will have a truly successful ending.

Remember that by the power of the Holy Spirit, your *old self* is dead and the *new self* has taken control of your thoughts and actions. Take what you've learned and the gifts you've been given and help "make disciples" of others. Help spread the good news of the gospel of Christ, and live out your life worshiping God instead of intoxicating chemicals.

Think About It

1. What role does personal responsibility play in addictive behaviors? Does your behavior correspond to that of a spiritually mature person?

2. How important is your environment in determining the quality of your choices? What roles do specific people play in your recovery? Are they positive or negative?

3. Which criminal do you most resemble in terms of your attitude toward God? Knowing that you will eventually face judgment, have you made a decision to follow Christ?

Pray About It

As you take time to pray a final time, here are a few ideas to get you started:

- Ask God to give you the strength to take a stand by achieving eternal salvation in Jesus Christ.
- Pray that Jesus becomes your personal Savior and that you will find your name written in the Book of Life.

- Thank God for helping you to conquer your addictions so that you may serve as an example to others in the spiritual fight against the Devil and addictive behaviors.

PRAYER OF SALVATION

The following is an example of a simple prayer of salvation. If you voice these words with passion and sincerity, your prayers will be answered, and you'll be born again. You may wish to pray to God in your own words, which might seem more natural to you. In the end, the words matter less than the desire of your heart.

> Father God, as I sit here alone in the shadow of my sins, I realize I've been running away from you all my life. I understand I was born into a fallen world and have been living a life of sin and selfishness all along. I know I've pushed you away by choosing to worship myself (and chemicals) instead of you. I want to turn away from the desires of my former life and the darkness within me that stained my soul.

> I surrender my life to your Son, Jesus. I believe He lived a sinless life and died a sinner's death on the cross. I understand He offered Himself as a sacrifice for every one of my sins, including those related to addiction. I believe He was resurrected and ascended to heaven, having paid the debt I owed for my many personal sins.

> Please help me conquer my addictive behaviors with the power and presence of your Holy Spirit. Give me a humble heart, and encourage me so that I may serve as an example to others. And finally, grant me the joy and miraculous peace of salvation in Jesus Christ. Amen.

Made in the USA
Middletown, DE
07 January 2023